United States Government Accountability Office

Report to Congressional Addressees

I0415850

April 2012

FARM BILL

Issues to Consider for Reauthorization

GAO

Accountability ★ Integrity ★ Reliability

GAO-12-338SP

Contents

Figures

Abbreviations

CAFO	concentrated animal feeding operation
CBO	Congressional Budget Office
DHS	Department of Homeland Security
E10	fuel blend containing approximately 10 percent ethanol
E15	fuel blend containing approximately 15 percent ethanol
EPA	Environmental Protection Agency
EQIP	Environmental Quality Incentives Program
HHS	Department of Health and Human Services
HSPD-9	Homeland Security Presidential Directive-9
HUD	Department of Housing and Urban Development
MSA	metropolitan statistical area
NPDRS	National Plant Disease Recovery System
SBA	Small Business Administration
SNAP	Supplemental Nutrition Assistance Program
SURE	Supplemental Revenue Assistance Program
USAID	U.S. Agency for International Development
USDA	U.S. Department of Agriculture
2008 Farm Bill	Food, Conservation, and Energy Act of 2008

United States Government Accountability Office
Washington, DC 20548

April 24, 2012

The Honorable Debbie Stabenow
Chairwoman
Committee on Agriculture, Nutrition and Forestry
United States Senate

The Honorable Frank Lucas
Chairman
The Honorable Collin Peterson
Ranking Member
Committee on Agriculture
House of Representatives

The Government Accountability Office (GAO) and the U.S. Department of Agriculture's Office of Inspector General (OIG) seek to enhance the efficiency, effectiveness, and accountability of the federal government. As Congress debates ways to address the federal government's long-term fiscal imbalance, it becomes even more critical that we help with this challenge by identifying opportunities for cost-savings and for improving programs to ensure that every dollar counts.

In this spirit and in anticipation of upcoming deliberations over the 2012 Farm Bill, we are issuing companion reports today. They present the following set of principles significant to the integrity, efficiency, and effectiveness of programs in the farm bill:

- *Relevance.* Does the program concern an issue of national interest? Is the program consistent with current statutes and international agreements? Have the domestic and international food and agriculture sectors changed significantly, or are they expected to change, in ways that affect the program's purpose?

- *Distinctiveness.* Is the program unique and free from overlap or duplication with other programs? Is it well-coordinated with similar programs?

- *Targeting.* Is the program's distribution of benefits consistent with contemporary assessments of need?

- *Affordability*. Is the program affordable, given the nation's severe budgetary constraints? Is it using the most efficient, cost-effective approaches?

- *Effectiveness*. Are program goals clear, with a direct connection to policies, resource allocations, and actions? Does the program demonstrate measurable progress toward its goals? Is it generally free of unintended consequences, including ecological, social, or economic effects? Does the program allow for adjustments to changes in markets?

- *Oversight*. Does the program have mechanisms, such as internal controls, to monitor compliance and help minimize fraud, waste, and abuse in areas where these are most likely to occur?

In the context of these principles, our reports summarize key GAO and OIG findings, respectively, related to farm bill programs. The principles could guide consideration of each program and potential program, and the summaries could help Congress make well-informed decisions about program design while continuing to maintain a strong agricultural sector and the safety and security of the nation's food supply and to provide nutrition assistance, promote U.S. exports, support renewable energy and conservation, and enhance economic growth in rural communities.

If you or your staff members have any questions about this report, please contact Lisa Shames, Director, Natural Resources and Environment, at (202) 512-3841 or shamesl@gao.gov. Contact points for our Offices of Congressional Relations and Public Affairs may be found on the last page of this report. GAO staff who made key contributions to this report are listed in appendix IV.

Gene L. Dodaro
Comptroller General
 of the United States

Section 1: Introduction

In the early 1930s, when farm foreclosures occurred every day and American agriculture was hit hard by drought and economic disaster, Congress enacted agricultural legislation to, among other things, protect farmers against the risks of low crop prices and bad weather. Since then, Congress has periodically passed farm bills to help farmers manage the risks that come with farming and has added programs through these bills that are to provide domestic and international food assistance, promote economic development in rural areas, and help advance alternatives to petroleum fuel, among other things.

The most recent farm bill—the Food, Conservation, and Energy Act of 2008 (2008 Farm Bill)—included a wide variety of programs, and its major provisions are expected to cost about $402 billion over 5 years, according to a 2010 estimate by the Congressional Research Service (CRS). As Congress prepares to pass a new farm bill in 2012, severe budget constraints are likely to shape deliberations. In the fall of 2011, as the Joint Select Committee on Deficit Reduction (joint committee) worked to identify ways to cut federal spending, Members of Congress, the administration, and several agricultural groups released proposals recommending modifications to farm bill programs, including potential areas for budget cuts. Many of the proposals target farm programs, which account for a significant amount of funding under the farm bill. The leadership of the House and Senate Agriculture Committees sent a letter to the joint committee recommending $23 billion in net deficit reduction from mandatory programs within their jurisdiction. Ultimately, the joint committee did not reach consensus on deficit reduction, but the dialogue it engendered might lay the groundwork for the upcoming debate over the design of the next farm bill.

We have previously reported that some farm bill programs offer opportunities for cost savings, could be delivered more efficiently and effectively, or may be working at cross purposes.[1] In this context, this report identifies principles we have found to be significant to integrity, effectiveness, and efficiency in farm bill programs since 2003, after much of the 2002 Farm Bill was implemented. Similarly, the Inspector General for the U.S. Department of Agriculture (USDA) has also reported findings and recommendations in these areas to strengthen farm bill programs. In

---

[1]For example, see GAO *Opportunities to Reduce Potential Duplication in Government Programs, Save Tax Dollars, and Enhance Revenue*, GAO-11-318SP (Washington, D.C.: Mar. 1, 2011).

a companion report, the Office of Inspector General adopts these principles and summarizes its work related to farm bill programs.[2]

To develop this list of principles, we first identified the universe of our reports issued from January 2003 through July 2011 that were potentially related to farm bill programs.[3] We screened these reports to exclude those that were not relevant and those that had no recommendations intended to improve the integrity, efficiency, or effectiveness of farm bill programs. We reviewed a subset of the relevant reports to develop a preliminary list of principles and then conducted a content analysis of all relevant reports to categorize findings by principle, refining the principles as we did so. We also reviewed some of our other products that examine governmentwide issues to inform our final list of principles.[4] The work for these reports was conducted in accordance with generally accepted government auditing standards. Those standards require that we plan and perform the audit to obtain sufficient, appropriate evidence to provide a reasonable basis for our findings and conclusions based on our audit objectives. We believe that the evidence obtained provided a reasonable basis for our findings and conclusions based on our audit objectives. In addition, we obtained comments on a draft of this report from USDA, which provided technical comments that we incorporated as appropriate. Appendix I contains more detailed information on our scope and methodology.

We conducted our work for this report from April 2011 through April 2012 in accordance with all sections of GAO's *Quality Assurance Framework* that are relevant to our objectives. The framework requires that we plan and perform the engagement to obtain sufficient and appropriate evidence to meet our stated objectives and to discuss any limitations in our work. We believe that the information and data obtained, and the analysis conducted, provide a reasonable basis for any findings and conclusions in this product.

---

[2]U.S. Department of Agriculture, Office of Inspector General, *Farm Bill: Issues to Consider for Reauthorization,* 50099-0001-10 (Washington D.C.: April 2012).

[3]We subsequently added some reports issued from August 2011 through March 2012 because they are relevant to farm bill deliberations.

[4]For example, GAO, *21st Century Challenges: Reexamining the Base of the Federal Government,* GAO-05-325SP (Washington, D.C.: February 2005).

Principles Identified as Significant to Integrity, Effectiveness, and Efficiency in Farm Bill Programs

Based on the review of our reports issued from January 2003 through March 2012 that were relevant to farm bill programs, we identified the following principles and associated key questions that could be applicable to Congress's deliberations for the 2012 Farm Bill:

- *Relevance.* Does the program concern an issue of national interest? Is the program consistent with current statutes and international agreements? Have the domestic and international food and agriculture sectors changed significantly, or are they expected to change, in ways that affect the program's purpose?

- *Distinctiveness.* Is the program unique and free from overlap or duplication with other programs? Is it well coordinated with similar programs?

- *Targeting.* Is the program's distribution of benefits consistent with contemporary assessments of need?

- *Affordability.* Is the program affordable, given the nation's severe budgetary constraints? Is it using the most efficient, cost-effective approaches?

- *Effectiveness.* Are program goals clear, with a direct connection to policies, resource allocations, and actions? Does the program demonstrate measurable progress toward its goals? Is it generally free of unintended consequences, including ecological, social, or economic effects? Does the program allow for adjustments to changes in markets?

- *Oversight.* Does the program have mechanisms, such as internal controls, to monitor compliance and help minimize fraud, waste, and abuse in areas where these are most likely to occur?

The 2008 Farm Bill consists of 15 titles and related provisions covering support for commodity crops, horticulture and livestock, conservation, nutrition, trade and food aid, agricultural research, farm credit, rural development, energy, forestry, and other related programs. For select farm bill titles, we summarized our findings in sections that correspond to farm bill titles and highlighted the relevant principles as they apply to these titles. The summaries relate to some, but not all, of the titles in the

2008 Farm Bill because since 2003, we have not produced a significant body of work concerning major provisions in every title.[5] Appendix II presents GAO reports related to titles in the 2008 Farm Bill that were issued from January 2003 through March 2012. Appendix III presents reports from the USDA Office of Inspector General, issued from October 2003 through February 2012, that the Office determined are relevant to titles in the 2008 Farm Bill.

Overview of Titles in the 2008 Farm Bill

The 2008 Farm Bill has governed many federal agriculture, food, and related programs since it was enacted into law in June 2008. It reauthorized, expanded, and modified many programs, amended laws, created new programs and initiatives, and repealed some programs. This farm bill enacted mandatory spending for commodity, crop insurance, nutrition assistance, conservation and trade programs. For other programs—including most rural development, research, and agricultural credit programs—the farm bill primarily authorized discretionary spending (i.e., spending subject to separate appropriations legislation). In 2011, the Congressional Budget Office (CBO) estimated that mandatory spending in the 2008 Farm Bill would cost about $95 billion annually from 2010 through 2012. Many of the bill's provisions expire at the end of fiscal year 2012. The following are summaries of the 2008 Farm Bill's titles, which are generally administered by USDA:

Title I: Commodity Programs. Under this title, the federal government provides assistance to farmers producing certain commodities, including wheat, feed grains, cotton, rice, oilseeds, and peanuts. Assistance is provided largely through three mechanisms: (1) direct payments unrelated to production or prices; (2) counter-cyclical payments for a commodity that are triggered when prices are below statutorily set targets; and (3) marketing assistance loans and loan deficiency payments; the latter occur when crop prices fall below statutorily set levels. In addition, support for the dairy industry is provided by, for example, having the government purchase dairy products and make payments to eligible farmers when milk prices fall below a certain level; and support for sugar growers and processors is provided by maintaining guaranteed minimum prices through a variety of mechanisms. In 2011,

---

[5]The 2008 Farm Bill titles without a corresponding summary include Title V (Credit), Title VIII (Forestry), Title X (Horticulture and Organic Agriculture), Title XI (Livestock), Title XIII (Commodity Futures), Title XIV (Miscellaneous), and Title XV (Trade and Tax Provisions).

CBO estimated that mandatory outlays in the commodity programs title would cost about $6 billion annually from 2010 through 2012.

Title II: Conservation. Farm bill conservation programs, generally administered by USDA, provide technical and financial assistance to farmers who voluntarily adopt conservation practices to mitigate the degradation of natural resources that can result from agriculture. For example, some conservation programs aim to prevent soil erosion, conserve and improve wildlife resources, protect wetlands, or protect water and air quality. Other conservation programs focus on specific restoration efforts, including those for the Chesapeake Bay and the Great Lakes Basin. In 2011, CBO estimated that mandatory outlays in the conservation title would cost about $5 billion annually from 2010 through 2012.

Title III: Trade. This title includes provisions related to international food assistance and trade. The 2008 Farm Bill reauthorizes the Food for Peace Act, which includes provisions for the largest U.S. international food assistance program, administered by the U.S. Agency for International Development (USAID).[6] In addition, the 2008 Farm Bill reauthorizes smaller food assistance programs, including Food for Progress, the Bill Emerson Humanitarian Trust, and the McGovern-Dole International School Feeding and Child Nutrition Program, all administered by USDA. The farm bill also adds a small pilot program that supports local and regional procurement of food assistance.

This title includes such trade provisions as export credit guarantees and export market development. Export credit guarantees ensure payments to U.S. financial institutions when foreign buyers finance their purchases of U.S. agricultural exports. Export market development programs promote the sale of U.S. agricultural exports overseas by supporting such activities as market research and consumer promotions. In 2011, CBO estimated that mandatory outlays in the trade title would cost about $287 million annually from 2010 through 2012.

Title IV: Nutrition. This title, which accounts for about two thirds of all spending mandated in the 2008 Farm Bill, includes programs to support

---

[6] In addition to reauthorizing the legislation, the 2008 Farm Bill changed the name of the original authorizing legislation from the Agricultural Trade Development and Assistance Act of 1954, commonly known as Public Law 480, to the Food for Peace Act and deleted export market development as one of the objectives of the programs.

domestic food and nutrition assistance. The largest of these programs is the Supplemental Nutrition Assistance Program (SNAP), which aims to help low income individuals and families obtain a better diet by supplementing their income with benefits to purchase food. School meal programs are authorized in other laws, but the farm bill includes some minor provisions related to the programs, such as a pilot project to purchase whole grains for use in school meals. In 2011, CBO estimated that major provisions in the nutrition title would cost about $76 billion annually in mandatory outlays from 2010 through 2012.

Title V: Credit. Under separate legislation, the federal government provides credit assistance for farmers through two lenders. USDA's Farm Service Agency makes loans to farmers who cannot otherwise qualify for credit and guarantees repayment of loans made by other lenders. In addition, a government-sponsored lender, the Farm Credit System, makes loans to creditworthy farmers. The 2008 Farm Bill made minor changes to the statutes for these two lenders. In 2011, CBO estimated that the combination of mandatory outlays and income from fees paid by banks would result in about $245 million in net receipts to the government annually from 2010 through 2012.

Title VI: Rural Development. This title includes programs that support rural housing, utilities, and economic development, through loans, grants, and technical and financial assistance for rural businesses and infrastructure development. It also sets priorities for expanding broadband service to underserved areas. In 2011, CBO estimated that mandatory outlays in the rural development title would cost about $30 million annually from 2010 through 2012.

Title VII: Research and Related Matters. Under this title, the federal government provides support for USDA's research and development programs, including research on food safety and nutrition, plant and animal health and production, agricultural economics, renewable energy, organic agriculture, and bioterrorism. Through these programs, USDA conducts research directly and provides grants for research conducted in universities and other institutions. In 2011, CBO estimated that mandatory outlays in the research and related matters title would cost about $69 million annually from 2010 through 2012.

Title VIII: Forestry. Many federal forestry programs are separately authorized and do not require reauthorization in the farm bill. However, some programs and provisions related to forestry—especially on private lands—are authorized or amended in the farm bill. For example, the 2008

Farm Bill directed the Secretary of Agriculture to create a new community forest and open space conservation program to acquire forests threatened with conversion for non-forest uses, added national priorities for funding private forest conservation, required states to develop and submit statewide assessments of forest resources to receive federal funding for the conservation of private forests, and amended existing law to restrict imports of illegally logged wood. In 2011, CBO estimated that mandatory outlays in the forestry title would cost about $10 million annually from 2010 through 2012.

Title IX: Energy. Under this title, the federal government provides support for programs that promote biofuels, biobased products, and ethanol production. These programs fund activities such as the construction of biofuel refineries, federal agency procurement of biobased products (e.g., corn-based plastics, soybean-based lubricants, and citrus-based cleaners), energy efficiency improvements, rural energy self sufficiency, studies on biofuels infrastructure needs, and efforts to encourage the use of *woody biomass* for energy production. *Woody biomass*—which includes material from trees and woody plants—can be used to generate energy for heating or cooling buildings, among other things. In 2011, CBO estimated that mandatory outlays in the energy title would cost about $358 million annually from 2010 through 2012.

Title X: Horticulture and Organic Agriculture. This title includes provisions that support state efforts to enhance competitiveness of specialty crops (i.e., fruits, vegetables, tree nuts, dried fruits, and nursery crops including floriculture), fund farmers' markets, help farmers with organic certification costs, and call for data collection on organic agriculture, among other things. In 2011, CBO estimated that mandatory outlays in the horticulture and organic agriculture title would cost about $102 million annually from 2010 through 2012.

Title XI: Livestock. Farm bills traditionally have not included price and income support programs for most animal agriculture (except dairy) as they have for major crops. The 2008 Farm Bill, however, introduced a new livestock title that modifies laws and requirements related to livestock, meat, poultry, and catfish. For example, it calls for enhancing electronic reporting of data on livestock markets, addresses concerns about livestock disease prevention and food safety, extends mandatory safety inspections to catfish, and allows some interstate sales of state-inspected meat and poultry. According to CBO, there are no mandatory outlays in the livestock title from 2010 through 2012.

Title XII: Crop Insurance and Disaster Assistance Programs. The federal crop insurance program does not require reauthorization in the farm bill, but the 2008 Farm Bill modified the program, which subsidizes the cost of farmers' premiums and pays an allowance to insurance companies to cover the administrative and operating expenses of selling and servicing crop insurance policies, among other things. The farm bill also provided support for disaster assistance programs in this title and in Title XV, the trade and tax provisions title. In 2011, CBO estimated that mandatory outlays in the crop insurance and disaster assistance programs title—as well as outlays for the disaster assistance program in the trade and tax provisions title—would cost about $7 billion annually from 2010 through 2012.

Title XIII: Commodity Futures. This title reauthorizes funding for the Commodity Futures Trading Commission, an independent regulatory agency, and further amends the Commodity Exchange Act. According to CBO, there are no mandatory outlays in the commodity futures title.

Title XIV: Miscellaneous. The miscellaneous title includes provisions affecting research, rural development, biosecurity, animal welfare, and socially disadvantaged farmers and ranchers, among other issues. In 2011, CBO estimated that mandatory outlays in the miscellaneous title would cost about $53 million annually from 2010 through 2012.

Title XV: Trade and Tax Provisions. This title creates a new disaster assistance program—Supplemental Revenue Assistance Program (SURE)—to compensate farmers for certain disaster-related losses, including those not covered by crop insurance. It also introduces numerous revenue and tax provisions affecting customs fees, conservation, and commodity program payments. According to CBO, the only mandatory outlays in the trade and tax provisions title are those for the SURE program, which CBO included in its estimates for the crop insurance and disaster assistance programs title.

Section 2: Commodity Programs

Commodity programs help protect farmers against risks such as declines in crop prices and support farm income.

The federal government spent over $6 billion on farm program payments to farmers in 2010. These payments go to both individuals and "entities," including corporations, partnerships, and estates. Some of these payments are tied to revenue or market changes—for example, payments may compensate farmers when crop prices go below a certain threshold—while others, called direct payments, are fixed annual payments based on farms' historic production. For each type of payment, statutory provisions define which farmers are eligible to receive payments and may limit the amount each farmer or entity can receive. For example, farmers whose incomes exceed statutorily defined caps are not eligible to receive payments. Nearly all of the farm policy proposals released in 2011 either reduce or eliminate direct payments.

The following are our key findings and applicable principles:

Reducing or Terminating Direct Payments Could Better Target Program Benefits and Save Tax Dollars

Applicable principles:
- Relevance
- Targeting
- Affordability
- Effectiveness

The following key findings may contribute to the conversation on the 2012 Farm Bill concerning direct payments:

- Farmers receive direct payments—fixed annual payments that are not influenced by risk factors such as market forces—even in years of record income; recipients of farm program payments have higher incomes, on average, than other tax filers. Direct payments are concentrated among the largest recipients because these payments are tied to land and paid on a per-acre basis (GAO-11-318SP).

- Direct payments were expected to be transitional when they were originally authorized in the 1996 Farm Bill, but subsequent farm bills have continued them. Proponents say they help the United States meet its commitments under international trade agreements, which set ceilings on government payments classified as trade-distorting. Unlike other farm program payments, direct payments are not tied to production levels or market prices, and are deemed to not distort international agricultural markets. The United States has classified direct payments as meeting related World Trade Organization rules. As a result, other farm program payments can be provided with a reduced risk of exceeding the ceilings. However, according to economists, this advantage has become less relevant recently because high crop prices, which are expected to continue through the foreseeable future, have kept farm program payments well below the ceiling on trade-distorting payments (GAO-11-318SP).

- Direct payments may compound challenges for beginning farmers. According to USDA studies, these and other farm payments result in higher prices to buy or rent land because in some cases the payments go directly to landowners—resulting in higher land value—and in other cases the payments go to tenants, prompting landlords to raise rents. In recent years, this effect has been most pronounced for direct payments because crop prices have not fallen below the threshold needed to trigger the other payments at significant levels. In 2010, direct payments accounted for about $5 billion and all other farm payments combined accounted for about $1 billion (GAO-11-318SP).

- Phasing out or terminating direct payments could result in savings of up to $5 billion per year (GAO-11-318SP).

USDA Has Increased Oversight to Reduce Potential Improper Payments, but Continued Vigilance Is Needed

Applicable principle:
- Oversight

The following key findings may contribute to the conversation on the 2012 Farm Bill concerning improper payments in farm programs:

- USDA paid nearly $50 million from 2003 through 2006 in farm program payments to thousands of individuals whose incomes exceeded the eligibility cap at that time—$2.5 million, making them potentially ineligible for farm program payments. These payments occurred primarily because USDA did not have management controls, such as reviews of an appropriate sample of recipients' tax returns, to verify that payments were going only to individuals who did not exceed the income eligibility caps (GAO-09-67). According to agency officials, in July 2009, USDA implemented management controls to address this issue. Consideration of individuals whose incomes exceed the eligibility limit continues to be an important issue as Congress designs the next farm bill.

- USDA paid $1.1 billion in farm program payments in the names of over 170,000 deceased farmers from 1999 through 2005. USDA regulations allow estates that meet certain conditions to receive payments after a farmer dies, but USDA did not determine whether the estates met those conditions. In addition, USDA relied on the heirs to an estate to inform USDA about whether a farmer receiving a payment was deceased. USDA could not be assured that millions of dollars in farm payments were proper because it did not have management controls to verify the status of individuals receiving payments (GAO-07-818). According to USDA officials, since 2007, they have been conducting data-matching tests with Social Security Administration records to verify that payment recipients are alive, and if they determine that a payment was inappropriate, they attempt to recover it. The agency did not, however, take steps to determine if it made improper payments before 2007 and if so, to recover the appropriate amounts.

- USDA made farm program payments to hundreds of individuals who may have had only limited involvement in farming because it lacked management controls to verify that payments went only to individuals who met eligibility requirements to be "actively engaged in farming." To meet this eligibility standard, an individual or entity must provide a significant contribution of inputs of capital, land, or equipment, as well as a significant contribution of services of personal labor or active personal management to the farming operation (GAO-04-407). USDA has since implemented some management controls to ensure that individuals meet the active-engagement-in-farming standard, but it still has not defined a measurable standard of what constitutes a significant contribution of active personal management. Doing so could help the agency ensure that individuals receiving farm program payments are not simply getting paid for allowing their name to be used on a farming operation document.

Section 3: Conservation

A strong U.S. agricultural sector benefits the economy and the health of the nation, but if improperly managed, agricultural production can lead to the degradation of natural resources. For example, every year, more than a billion tons of soil erode from the nation's cropland, and thousands of other acres, including wetlands, are converted into new cropland. Because farmers and ranchers own and manage about 940 million acres, or about half of the continental United States' land area, they are among the most important stewards of our soil, water, and wildlife habitat.

To address the potential for the degradation of natural resources, Congress has authorized over 20 agricultural conservation programs in farm bills and in other legislation. These programs aim, among other things, to reduce soil erosion, enhance water quality and supplies, and improve wildlife habitat. To support these goals, USDA provides financial and technical assistance for farmers to adopt specific conservation practices.

Some conservation programs pay farmers to remove land from agricultural production to achieve environmental benefits. The largest of these programs, the Conservation Reserve Program, reimburses farmers for removing land from production for at least 10 years at a time. The Grassland Reserve Program pays farmers to maintain or restore grasslands, which help to maintain and improve water quality. However, grasslands are often converted to cropland by farmers (particularly in the northern plains) to garner the benefits of agricultural production. Another conservation program, the Environmental Quality Incentives Program (EQIP), is intended to promote agricultural production, forest management, and environmental quality as compatible goals by, among other things, encouraging producers to use management practices that support environmental goals. Conservation programs also pay farmers to control pollution generated by concentrated animal-feeding operations (CAFO)—large operations that raise livestock and poultry in a confined situation. The Environmental Protection Agency (EPA) is responsible for regulating air and water pollutants, including those from CAFOs, and requires CAFOs that discharge certain pollutants to obtain a permit.

Another conservation program aims to restore soil, air, and related resources in the Chesapeake Bay watershed, where agricultural runoff is the single largest source of pollutants, according to EPA. In 2009, the President issued an executive order establishing the Federal Leadership Committee to oversee the development and coordination of federal restoration programs and activities and called for the development of a strategy to protect and restore the bay. The Federal Leadership Committee—chaired by the EPA Administrator, and including senior representatives from USDA and the departments of Commerce, Defense, Homeland Security, the Interior, and Transportation—issued the *Strategy for Protecting and Restoring the Chesapeake Bay Watershed* (*Strategy*) in May 2010.

Figure 1 shows one conservation practice—*strip cropping*—that is used in some conservation programs to reduce soil erosion. Strip cropping involves the precise arrangement of alternating strips in a field. The crops are arranged so that all strips of grass or close-growing crops are alternated with a clean-tilled strip or a strip with less protective cover.

Figure 1: Strip Cropping to Reduce Soil Erosion

Source: Photo courtesy of USDA Natural Resources Conservation Service.

Note: *Strip cropping* means growing row crops, forages, or small grains in equal-width strips.

The following are our key findings and applicable principles:

USDA Should Ensure Farm and Conservation Programs Do Not Work at Cross Purposes or Duplicate Efforts

Applicable principles:
- Distinctiveness
- Effectiveness

The following key findings may contribute to the conversation on the 2012 Farm Bill concerning farm and conservation programs:

- Some farm and conservation programs may work at cross-purposes, undermining the effectiveness of a conservation program. Specifically, some farmers choose to maintain grassland or convert cropland to grassland, but others do the opposite—convert grassland to cropland—and in both scenarios, farmers may receive federal payments under the statutes. For example, according to USDA, from 1997 through 2007, roughly 1.57-million acres of cropland in the Northern Plains region were converted to grassland, and during the same period about 2.22-million acres of grassland were converted to cropland in the region. This conversion to cropland in the region accounted for about 57 percent of total grassland-to-cropland conversions nationwide during the period (GAO-07-1054). In 2011, USDA issued a bulletin describing new eligibility requirements for participating in the federal crop insurance program when croplands have recently been converted from grasslands. GAO believes that this guidance will help prevent the conversion of grassland to cropland.

- Farm program payments are a major factor in farmers' decisions to convert native grassland to cropland, according to our analysis and other economic studies. Farm program payments continue to be relevant because they reduce farmers' financial risks and, in many cases, increase their profits over maintaining grassland. We also recognized that other factors, such as high crop prices, may also influence farmers' decisions on whether to keep their land as grassland or convert it to cropland (GAO-07-1054). We recommended that USDA study and report on the issue of conversions of grassland to cropland, and it did so in 2011. USDA's study included an analysis of the role of farm programs in farmers' decisions to convert grasslands to cropland. Conversion of native grassland to cropland remains a concern as Congress designs the next farm bill.

- Some of USDA's conservation programs have duplicative program goals and overlapping eligibility requirements, which can make certain conservation practices eligible for payments under multiple programs. To reduce the potential for duplicate payments, Congress and USDA have instituted legislative and regulatory measures, but we found that some duplicate payments were still made (GAO-06-312). In March 2009, USDA officials told us they had developed a process to preclude such payments from being made, but the broader issue of overlapping program goals remains.

Procedures for Allocating Funds and Enforcing Compliance Could Be Improved to Better Promote Conservation Program Goals

Applicable principles:
- Targeting
- Effectiveness
- Oversight

The following key findings may contribute to the conversation on the 2012 Farm Bill concerning conservation goals:

- In 2006, USDA's formula for allocating funds to states under EQIP was not clearly linked to the program's goal of optimizing environmental benefits. Specifically, because the department did not have a documented rationale for including each of the factors and weights used in the formula, it was not clear whether the program was effectively targeting states with the most significant environmental concerns arising from agricultural production. For example, the formula uses a factor to address the waste management costs of small-animal-feeding operations but not such costs for large-animal-feeding operations, which can also damage the environment and might be more prevalent in some states than others (GAO-06-969). Beginning with its fiscal year 2009 funding allocations, USDA modified some elements in the formula and documented its rationale for all of the elements, and these actions addressed our recommendation.

- USDA developed long-term, outcome-oriented performance measures for the EQIP program but does not use performance assessment results to inform revisions to the funding allocation formula. Doing so could help ensure that funds continue to be directed to the highest priority areas, even as conditions change (GAO-06-969). In January 2012, USDA officials told us they had taken steps to incorporate performance considerations into EQIP funding allocation decisions. We are currently evaluating whether the changes address our concerns.

- According to our nationwide survey, almost half of USDA's field offices did not implement farm-bill conservation compliance provisions as required, in part because the offices reported that they were uncomfortable with their enforcement role. Some field office staff said it was difficult to cite farmers for noncompliance in the small communities where the staff and farmers both live and work. Furthermore, their noncompliance decisions were waived about 61 percent of the time, and the waiver decisions were not always adequately justified, providing further disincentive for issuing noncompliance decisions (GAO-03-418). In response to our recommendation, USDA took some steps from 2003 through 2007 to improve field offices' implementation of the compliance review process, but some environmentalists have recently questioned whether the agency is adequately enforcing conservation compliance. The agency has not changed its process for justifying waiver determinations.

Agencies Need to More Effectively Address Potential Impacts Resulting from Agricultural Runoff and Other Sources

Applicable principles:
- Distinctiveness
- Effectiveness

The following key findings may contribute to the conversation on the 2012 Farm Bill concerning agricultural runoff and other pollutants:

- In 2010, the Federal Leadership Committee issued a strategy for restoring the Chesapeake Bay, which has been in decline primarily because excess nutrients enter the bay from agricultural runoff and other sources, such as population growth and development. However, the strategy's goals and actions may not be achieved, in part because not all bay restoration stakeholders are working toward the same goals. State officials told us that they are not working toward the *Strategy's* goals, in part because they view the *Strategy* as a federal document. Instead, most state bay restoration work is conducted according to state commitments made in a previous bay restoration agreement. The *Strategy* and the previous agreement goals are somewhat similar, but they also differ. For example, both call for managing fish species, but the *Strategy* identifies brook trout as a key species for restoration and the previous agreement does not. The likelihood of achieving the goals is further reduced because the federal agencies do not plan to identify milestones for the entire restoration effort outlined in the committee's strategy. Instead, the agencies plan to create 2-year milestones for measuring progress made toward the *Strategy's* goals, with the first milestone covering 2012 and 2013. Without either aligning the goals of all watershed stakeholders or creating milestones for the entire effort, the federal agencies and states may not be able to gauge whether actions are leading to progress in achieving program goals (GAO-11-802).

- CAFOs have improved the efficiency of animal production, but the large amounts of manure they produce—sometimes over 1-million tons per year—can potentially pollute the air and water, and EPA has not assessed any resulting impacts to human health and the environment because it lacks key data. Specifically, EPA does not have data on the amount of pollutants that CAFOs are discharging, and even more fundamentally, on the number, location, and size of the operations to which it issues permits for discharging pollutants (GAO-08-944). In October 2011, EPA proposed a regulation to collect facility-specific information for a national inventory of CAFOs. In addition, by June 2012, the agency plans to develop methodologies to estimate the amount of air pollutants emitted by CAFOs. Once EPA's planned actions are completed, we will assess whether they address our concerns.

Section 4: Trade

In 2010, the United Nations' Food and Agriculture Organization estimated that a total of 925 million people worldwide are undernourished. The food and fuel crisis of 2006—2008 and the current global economic downturn exacerbated food insecurity in many developing countries and sparked food protests and riots in dozens of them. The United States provided nearly $2.3 billion to provide a total of 2.5-million metric tons of food aid commodities to food-insecure countries in fiscal year 2010. This amount accounted for about half of all global food aid supplies, making the United States the single largest donor of food aid.

U.S. international food assistance is delivered through multiple programs, some of which were authorized or amended in farm bills. The programs, administered mainly by the U.S. Agency for International Development (USAID) and USDA, serve a range of objectives, including improving food security and supporting economic development. For example, the 2008 Farm Bill authorized $2.5 billion annually for USAID's Food for Peace program, which provides U.S. agricultural commodities to developing countries to help meet certain emergency and nonemergency food needs. A portion of these commodities—worth more than $300 million in 2010— are sold to generate funds for economic development activities, a practice known as *monetization. Monetization* originated when the U.S. government owned a surplus of agricultural commodities, but the United States now purchases commodities from the commercial market and ships them abroad, where partners sell them in another market to generate cash to fund development activities. USAID and USDA are required to ensure that monetization transactions do not have adverse market impacts—such as displacing commercial trade and discouraging local food production—in recipient countries. To help avoid such impacts, the agencies and their implementing partners conduct market assessments that recommend the maximum volume of commodities that can be monetized without displacing commercial trade or creating disincentives for local food production.

The 2008 Farm Bill also reauthorized an international school feeding program; authorized up to $22 million annually to USAID to improve, monitor, and evaluate the effectiveness and efficiency of nonemergency food assistance programs; and created a small pilot program for local or regional purchase and distribution of food assistance, which some experts say enables beneficiaries to receive food more quickly and cost effectively.

Even with a 1996 pledge by the United States and more than 180 world leaders to halve the number of undernourished people in the world by

2015, efforts by host governments and donors to achieve this goal have thus far been insufficient. In 2008, we reported that meeting this goal in sub-Saharan Africa (the region with the highest prevalence of food insecurity) was increasingly unlikely and that the United States' lack of a comprehensive strategy may have led to missed opportunities to leverage expertise and minimize overlap and duplication (GAO-08-680). Consistent with our recommendation, the administration issued a governmentwide global food security strategy in May 2010.

The following are our key findings and applicable principles:

U.S. Agencies Should Take Steps to Mitigate Risks Associated with Implementing the Governmentwide Global Food Security Strategy

Applicable principles:
- Effectiveness
- Oversight

The following key findings may contribute to the conversation on the 2012 Farm Bill concerning global food security:

- In 2010, 10 U.S. agencies supported a wide variety of programs and activities for global food security,[1] but the agencies lacked a common data system to effectively implement the governmentwide global food security strategy, which was issued in May 2010. Such a data system would include a commonly accepted definition of global food security programs and activities so that agencies could track expenditures and activities related to global food security (GAO-10-352). Without a common data system, the United States may be less able to oversee the effective implementation of the new strategy.

- The governmentwide global food security strategy is vulnerable to risks associated with the strategy's host government-led approach. Specifically, host governments generally have weak capacity, which can limit their ability to increase spending for agriculture, absorb significant increases in donor funding, and sustain donor-funded efforts over time. U.S. agencies may also be constrained in their efforts to strengthen the host government's capacity because these agencies have a shortage of expertise in agriculture and food security. Also, differences in policy priorities between donors, including the United States and host governments, could further complicate efforts to align donor assistance with host government strategies and hence

---

[1]These 10 U.S. agencies are USAID, Millennium Challenge Corporation, Department of the Treasury, USDA; the Department of State, the Department of Defense, U.S. Trade and Development Agency, Peace Corps, Office of the U.S. Trade Representative, and Office of Management and Budget.

potentially reduce the effectiveness of the new strategy (GAO-10-352). According to agency officials, they are taking steps to mitigate these risks, and we are continuing to monitor their efforts.

The Efficiency of International Food Assistance Programs Can Be Improved

Applicable principles:
- Affordability
- Effectiveness

The following key findings may contribute to the conversation on the 2012 Farm Bill concerning the efficiency of international food assistance programs:

- Inefficiencies in the monetization process—selling food assistance commodities to generate funds for economic development—reduced funding available to the U.S. government and its implementing partners for development projects by $219 million over 3 years (2008 through 2010 for USAID and 2007 through 2009 for USDA). The process of using cash to procure, ship, and sell commodities resulted in $503 million available for development projects out of the $722 million expended. Proceeds generated through monetization are less than what the U.S. government spends to buy and ship the commodities; as a result, the U.S. government does not fully recover its costs. USAID's average cost recovery, the ratio between the proceeds from sales and the cost of procuring and shipping the commodities, was 76 percent, while USDA's was 58 percent (GAO-11-636).

- Local or regional purchase of food in host countries can save money and delivery time in emergency situations, and as a result, it can be more cost-effective than in-kind food aid from the United States. However, concerns persist about the quality of the food and adherence to certain product specifications, raising questions about the program's effectiveness in ensuring food safety and nutritional content (GAO-09-570). In response to our recommendation, USAID and USDA have efforts under way to improve guidance for local or regional purchases that include commodity quality standards and to collect evidence on adherence to these standards.

- Food aid transportation and other delivery costs are requiring a larger share of program resources at the expense of procuring more food to feed hungry people, according to USAID officials (GAO-09-977SP). In 2007, we reported that despite growing demand for food aid, rising business and transportation costs contributed to a 52 percent decline in average tonnage delivered over a 5-year period—reducing the cost-effectiveness of the program (GAO-07-560). One factor contributing to high transportation costs is cargo preference laws that require 75 percent of food aid to be shipped on U.S.-flag carriers, which are generally more expensive than foreign-flag carriers. From fiscal years 2008 through 2010, cargo preference potentially cost the nonemergency food aid programs approximately $30 million (GAO-11-636).

Better Practices Offer Opportunities to Enhance the Effectiveness of International Food Assistance

Applicable principles:
- Targeting
- Affordability
- Effectiveness

The following key findings may contribute to the conversation on the 2012 Farm Bill concerning the effectiveness of international food assistance programs:

- USAID and USDA cannot ensure that monetization will avoid adverse market impacts—such as discouraging local food production and displacing commercial trade—in part because the market assessments the agencies conduct are weak and in part because the agencies do not assess the effects of monetization. Without better assessments, the agencies lack important information, including whether selling U.S. food causes the prices of similar foods in the host country to be depressed and creates disincentives for local producers, which could work against the agricultural development goals for which the funding was originally provided (GAO-11-636).

- Food rations designed for short-term emergencies are often used to address long-term food insecurity, but such rations do not always meet the nutritional needs of recipients if they rely solely on food aid. On the contrary, recipients can develop serious micronutrient deficiencies under these circumstances. For example, epidemics of scurvy (a severe vitamin C deficiency) have broken out among food aid beneficiaries who totally depended on food aid. Nevertheless, more than half of Food for Peace emergency funding was spent on multiyear programs, highlighting the need for guidance on how to address nutritional deficiencies that emerge during protracted emergencies (GAO-11-491).

- Newly developed specialized foods have the potential to better meet the nutritional needs of vulnerable groups, such as pregnant women and young children, but these foods are difficult to target to the intended recipients and more costly than conventional food aid, and their efficacy is still being tested. Because of the high costs combined with the lack of information, U.S. agencies face challenges with the trade-off between reaching more beneficiaries and increasing effectiveness at achieving nutritional outcomes for targeted groups (GAO-11-491).

- U.S. agencies and their implementing partners face difficulties targeting foods to the appropriate groups or individuals because (1) needs assessments only provide some of the required information and therefore are not always useful and (2) targeting can be undermined at the recipient level by the cultural practice of sharing among or within households. For example, in a household with one qualifying family member—defined as a child under 5 or a pregnant or lactating woman—the head of household said the specialized food is shared with the whole family, especially elderly members and the male head of household, who needs extra energy to work in the field (GAO-11-491).

- USAID's actions to improve its monitoring and evaluation of nonemergency food aid programs could be hindered by weak planning. Monitoring is essential to ensuring that these programs are implemented as intended, and evaluation helps ensure that they achieve their goal of reducing global food insecurity (GAO-09-980). Also, USDA provides weak performance monitoring of its international school feeding program, making it difficult to assess any progress made toward the program's objectives of education, nutrition, and sustainability. For example, the department's guidance does not have performance indicators to directly measure nutritional progress. Furthermore, USDA has not evaluated completed projects associated with this program, but according to agency officials, it is taking steps to do so. Specifically, for multiyear projects that began in 2010 or later, USDA now requires completed projects to be evaluated; the agency expects the first round of these evaluations to be issued in 2014 (GAO-11-544).

Section 5: Nutrition

The federal government spends billions of dollars every year on food and nutrition assistance programs, and millions of Americans turn to these federal programs when they lack the money to get enough to eat. The recent economic crisis has increased the number of people who are eligible for such assistance, with participation in the largest food assistance program—the Supplemental Nutrition Assistance Program (SNAP)—increasing by 33 percent between 2009 and 2011.

A complex network of 18 food assistance programs emerged piecemeal over the past several decades, through multiple pieces of legislation, including farm bills, to meet various needs.[1] For example, SNAP was reauthorized in the 2008 Farm Bill and provided more than $70 billion in benefits to low income individuals and households in 2011.[2]

USDA and the states jointly administer SNAP; USDA pays the full cost of benefits and seeks to ensure that states administer the program in compliance with program rules; the states determine whether households are eligible and issue benefits to participants through electronic debit cards. Participants use the cards to purchase food in authorized retail stores. However, every year, SNAP participants exchange hundreds of millions of dollars in benefits for cash instead of food with authorized retailers across the country, a practice known as trafficking. In a typical trafficking situation, a retailer gives a SNAP participant a discounted amount of cash—commonly 50 cents on the dollar—in exchange for SNAP benefits and pockets the difference. In addition, benefits are paid incorrectly each year when, for example, ineligible individuals receive benefits or eligible individuals are paid more or less than they are entitled to receive. In 2010, these payment errors—including overpayments and underpayments—amounted to more than $2 billion.

---

[1] The federal government currently funds close to 70 programs that are permitted to provide at least some support for domestic food assistance. Eighteen of these programs focus primarily on providing food and nutrition assistance to low income individuals and households.

[2] In October 1, 2008, a provision in the farm bill changed the name of the Food Stamp Program to the Supplemental Nutrition Assistance Program (SNAP). In this report, we discuss information related to both the Food Stamp Program and SNAP; however, for simplicity, we generally refer to both programs as SNAP.

The following are our key findings and applicable principles:

Agencies Need to Reduce Administrative Overlap among Domestic Food Assistance Programs

Applicable principles:
- Distinctiveness
- Effectiveness

The following key findings may contribute to the conversation on the 2012 Farm Bill concerning potential overlap among domestic food and nutrition assistance programs:

- Domestic food and nutrition assistance is provided through a decentralized system of primarily 18 different federal programs that show signs of overlap and inefficient use of resources. For example, applicants seeking assistance from multiple programs are often required to submit separate applications for each program and provide similar information verifying, for example, household income. By targeting various needs, the 18 food assistance programs help increase access to food for vulnerable populations, according to agency officials, but overlapping requirements can create unnecessary work for both providers and applicants and may result in the use of more administrative resources than needed. Simplifying, streamlining, or better aligning eligibility procedures and criteria across programs could result in sizable administrative cost savings, but such actions would need to be balanced against the goal of ensuring access to benefits for eligible individuals (GAO-10-346 and GAO-11-318SP).

- Not enough is known about the effectiveness of many of the domestic food and nutrition assistance programs. Research suggests that participation in 7 of the 18 programs—including 4 of the largest—is associated with positive health and nutrition outcomes consistent with program goals, such as raising the level of nutrition among low-income households. Yet, little is known about the effectiveness of the remaining 11 smaller programs because they have not been well studied. Without such information, it is difficult to determine whether these programs are filling an important gap or unnecessarily duplicating functions and services of other programs (GAO-10-346 and GAO-11-318SP).

USDA Could Benefit from Increased Attention to Food Program Integrity

Applicable principles:
- Affordability
- Oversight

The following key findings may contribute to the conversation on the 2012 Farm Bill concerning the integrity of the Supplemental Nutrition Assistance Program (SNAP):

- The national rate of SNAP trafficking declined from about 3.8 cents per dollar of benefits redeemed in 1993 to about 1.0 cent per dollar from 2006 through 2008. However, even at that lower rate, USDA estimates that about $330 million in SNAP benefits were trafficked annually in those 3 years because of program vulnerabilities, including limited oversight. For example, USDA authorizes some stores that have only limited food supplies to ensure access to food for some participants but may not inspect these stores again for 5 years after their initial authorization. Also, some states actively pursue and disqualify recipients who traffic their benefits while inaction by other states allows recipients suspected of trafficking to continue the practice (GAO-10-956T and GAO-07-53). The 2008 Farm Bill expanded USDA's authority to impose higher financial penalties for trafficking. In February 2012, USDA announced that it would soon publish a proposed rule strengthening penalties for retailers who commit fraud. According to USDA officials, the agency also made changes to its authorization process for some stores and now inspects higher-risk stores more frequently—some as often as once a year.

- The national payment error rate—the percentage of SNAP benefit dollars overpaid or underpaid to program participants—declined by about 57 percent from 2000 to 2010, from 8.91 percent to 3.81 percent, according to USDA. This reduction occurred in a time of increasing participation and is due, in part, to steps taken by USDA and states to reduce improper payments, such as increasing oversight and providing financial incentives and penalties based on performance. Despite this progress, the amount of benefits paid in error is substantial. The 3.8 percent error rate in 2010 totaled about $2.5 billion and necessitates continued top-level attention and commitment to determining the causes of improper payments and taking corrective actions to reduce them (GAO-10-956T).

Section 6: Rural Development

The federal government has provided assistance to eligible residents of rural America since the 1930s, when most of these residents worked on farms, and rural residents were generally poorer than urban residents. Such assistance is still available for these residents; however, the rural America of today is different from the rural America of the 1930s, and the distinctions between rural and urban life have blurred. For example, universal access to the Internet via broadband technologies—commonly referred to as broadband Internet access—is now considered a critical economic engine and a central component of 21st-century news and entertainment in rural as well as urban areas.

Multiple federal agencies—such as the Department of Commerce, the Small Business Administration (SBA), the Department of Housing and Urban Development (HUD), and USDA—administer economic development programs. Some economic development programs are targeted to rural areas and were addressed in the 2008 Farm Bill. USDA's rural development programs address the diverse and unique needs of rural America through loans, loan guarantees, and grants for public facilities and services, such as electricity and water systems. In addition, over 80 economic development programs, which sometimes target benefits to rural areas, support nine separate economic development activities, such as entrepreneurial efforts, infrastructure, and telecommunications.

The 2008 Farm Bill extended funding for some rural and economic development activities, such as water sanitation and wastewater projects. It also broadened eligibility for the farm labor housing program, clarified eligibility for rural utility loans, and authorized loans and loan guarantees for improving access to broadband services in rural areas.

The following are our key findings and applicable principles:

Agencies Need to Take Steps to Avoid Duplication, Overlap, and Fragmentation in Economic Development Programs

Applicable principles:
- Distinctiveness
- Affordability
- Effectiveness

The following key findings may contribute to the conversation on the 2012 Farm Bill concerning potential overlap or fragmentation of economic development programs:

- Each of over 80 economic development programs overlaps with at least one other program. To address the potential for problems that can result from overlap and fragmentation, we have identified collaborative practices agencies should consider. These practices include defining and articulating common outcomes for some of their related programs. USDA, the Department of Commerce, HUD, and SBA appear to have implemented some of these collaborative practices, but do not appear to have developed compatible policies or procedures, or identified opportunities to leverage resources with their federal partners, mainly because there are few incentives to collaborate and insufficient guidance on effective collaboration. For example, 52 different programs fund "entrepreneurial efforts," but any collaboration among the programs that we assessed occurred only on a case-by-case basis. Without finding ways to collaborate more, agencies may miss opportunities to leverage each other's strengths to more effectively promote economic development and use taxpayer dollars efficiently (GAO-11-318SP). Recently, three of the four agencies have taken initial steps to implement at least one of the collaborative practices, but they have provided limited evidence that they have taken steps to develop compatible policies or procedures (GAO-12-453SP).

- Agencies do not have key information on program outcomes, information that they need to determine whether potential overlap and fragmentation is resulting in ineffective or inefficient programs. For example, USDA officials stated that they have taken steps to ensure that the agency has data to measure the accomplishments of one of its largest rural development programs—the Business and Industry loan program—which was funded at approximately $53 million in fiscal year 2010, but it is unclear whether these data will provide the information needed to determine potential overlap. Without quality data, agencies may not be able to efficiently manage their programs, and Congress and others may not have information to help them identify opportunities for consolidating or eliminating some programs (GAO-11-318SP).

- Up to seven different federal agencies—including USDA and EPA—administer programs to improve access to safe drinking water and sanitation systems in the U.S.-Mexico border region, but their efforts have been ineffective, in part, because they have not developed coordinated policies and procedures. For example, EPA and USDA each provided funds to develop separate designs for a wastewater project serving the same community. When the community selected the USDA design, the need for the EPA design was eliminated, resulting in a waste of those federal funds. In another example, the lack of coordination among agencies resulted in a $900,000 investment of federal funds for pipes to distribute water, but these pipes are not usable because the water supply is insufficient (GAO-11-318SP and GAO-10-126).

- The United States has not achieved its goal of universal access to broadband largely because of the low profitability of infrastructure deployment in underserved areas, most of which are rural, according to industry stakeholders. The American Recovery and Reinvestment Act of 2009 authorized $7.2 billion for multiple agencies to increase broadband availability by developing a national broadband plan, mapping nationwide availability, and deploying infrastructure. Because the agencies have overlapping responsibilities that target the same population, it will be important for them to coordinate their efforts, particularly in specifying roles and responsibilities, to prevent duplication or fragmentation of efforts (GAO-09-494). In 2010, the Federal Communications Commission released a national broadband plan.

USDA Should Reconsider the Definition of "Rural" to Ensure Consistency with Program Purposes

Applicable principles:
- Targeting
- Effectiveness

The following key findings may contribute to the conversation on the 2012 Farm Bill concerning the definition of rural development programs:

- USDA used a definition of "rural" to determine eligibility for housing assistance in rural areas, but the use of this definition resulted in inconsistent determinations about which areas would receive program funds. For example, in 2004 we reported that the agency used a public road outside Hagerstown, Maryland, as the dividing line for determining eligibility for rural communities, resulting in apparently similar rural areas receiving different designations. In addition, statutory requirements for program eligibility may not reflect changes in rural areas or best determine which areas qualify for USDA housing programs. For example, we found the requirement that rural communities not be part of metropolitan statistical areas (MSA) to be of marginal utility. MSAs, which are defined as counties associated with a city or urbanized area that has a population of at least 50,000, are not intended to be urban-rural classifications and can contain both urban and rural areas. We suggested that changes to this requirement, such as using density measures rather than the MSA criterion, might allow USDA to better differentiate between urban and rural areas (GAO-05-110). In addition to our suggested alternative, Congress incorporated into the 2008 Farm Bill a requirement that USDA report on the various program definitions of "rural." USDA has not yet issued such a report. However, according to agency officials, USDA recently provided training to field staff to help address concerns about inconsistent eligibility determinations for rural areas.

Figure 2: Road Near Hagerstown, Maryland, That Divides a "Rural" Area" from a "Nonrural" Area, 2004

Source: GAO.

- USDA applied a "once a borrower, always a borrower" standard for distributing rural utility loans, which allows borrowers to continuously receive USDA assistance regardless of the extent of population increases within their service territories. As a result, these loans did not always target funds to rural areas where the need is greatest. In particular, loans went to recipients that provided utility services in over half the counties in the country that were classified as metropolitan, and 9.4 percent of all the counties had populations greater than

1 million. In the immediate vicinity of Atlanta, three cooperatives that provide service received a total of over $400 million in rural utility loans from 1999 through 2003. Without specifying that criteria apply to both initial and subsequent loans, the agency may not be able to target funds to rural areas (GAO-04-647). We suggested that Congress consider specifying that the program criterion for rural areas applies to both an initial loan and any subsequent loans that borrowers seek, but it did not follow our suggestion.

Section 7: Research and Related Matters

The U.S. agricultural system generates over $1 trillion in economic activity annually, and the entry of foreign pests and disease into this system can harm the economy, the environment, plant and animal health, and public health. USDA estimates that these biological invaders cost the American economy tens of billions of dollars annually in lower crop values, eradication programs, and emergency payments to farmers.

In part, to protect agriculture from the threats posed by foreign pests and disease, the 2008 Farm Bill provided over $300 million for 5 years to USDA for various research projects, according to estimates from the Congressional Research Service.[1] In addition, the 2008 Farm Bill authorized funding to support biosecurity planning and response in the United States, and more specifically, for activities that are to

- reduce the vulnerability of the U.S. food and agricultural system to chemical or biological attacks,

- continue partnerships with institutions to enhance U.S. biosecurity,

- make competitive grants for research on counterbioterrorism, and

- counter or otherwise respond to chemical or biological attacks.

In 2002, the Department of Homeland Security (DHS) was charged with coordinating U.S. federal efforts to, among other things, protect against agroterrorism—the deliberate introduction of animal and plant diseases—and USDA's main agricultural inspection mission was subsequently transferred to DHS. USDA retains some responsibility for the agricultural inspection programs, such as developing and issuing an inspection policy. USDA is also responsible for preventing the spread of Avian Influenza (AI) in poultry, with DHS taking the lead role in coordinating the federal response.

In 2004, the President issued Homeland Security Presidential Directive-9 (HSPD-9) to establish a national policy to defend the food and agriculture systems against terrorist attacks, major disasters, and other emergencies. Part of USDA's efforts to implement HSPD-9 include developing the National Plant Disease Recovery System (NPDRS) to help the nation

---

[1] Congressional Research Service, *Actual Farm Bill Spending and Cost Estimates*, (Dec. 13, 2010)

recover from high-consequence plant disease outbreaks that could devastate the nation's productions of economically important crops.

Furthermore, various legislation and presidential directives have called for a robust and integrated biosurveillance capability (i.e., the ability to provide early detection and situational awareness of potentially catastrophic biological events).

The following are our key findings and applicable principles:

Enhanced Oversight and Coordination Is Needed to Protect Agriculture from Terrorist Acts and Other Major Emergencies

Applicable principles:
- Distinctiveness
- Oversight

The following key findings may contribute to the conversation on the 2012 Farm Bill concerning how to defend agriculture:

- There is no centralized coordination effort to oversee the federal government's overall progress in implementing the nation's food and agriculture defense policy. Because several agencies have responsibilities outlined in HSPD-9, centralized oversight is important to avoid fragmentation and efficiently use scarce funds. For example, the Homeland Security Council previously collected and consolidated information from agencies, such as USDA, EPA, and the Department of Health and Human Services (HHS), on their efforts to implement their HSPD-9 responsibilities, information that agency officials considered useful. However, this practice stopped in late 2008 or early 2009, according to agency officials. Without coordinated activities to oversee agencies' HSPD-9 implementation efforts, federal decision makers may not have critical information they need to assess how well the nation is prepared for major emergencies and how efficiently agencies are using federal resources to prepare (GAO-11-652).

- Numerous federal agencies—such as USDA, DHS, and HHS—have biosurveillance responsibilities, and some have developed high-level strategies for their respective biodefense missions, but there is no comprehensive national strategy that integrates all agencies and capabilities. For example, USDA developed a strategy for the National Animal Health Surveillance System to help the agency pursue its own animal health mission, but the strategy is not intended to support an integrated national biosurveillance capability. Similarly, officials in various agencies have taken the lead to fulfill their agencies' biosurveillance missions, but they lack authority to direct other agencies with which they must partner to take specific action. Officials from multiple agencies stated that having a focal point would help coordinate federal efforts to develop a national biosurveillance capability (GAO-10-645). Consideration of a national biosurveillance capability continues to be a challenge.

- USDA's plans did not include DHS in the lead coordinating role for responding to an outbreak of avian influenza, even though DHS may be required to direct a federal response if the president declared a major disaster. Unless USDA and DHS work diligently together to define and understand roles and responsibilities in advance of a significant outbreak of avian influenza, delay could occur at the federal level as the two agencies attempt to work out their relationship during a time of crisis (GAO-07-652). According to agency officials, DHS and USDA have been working to develop a framework to guide federal-to-federal assistance during agriculture emergencies.

- Poor coordination between DHS and USDA under the Agriculture Quarantine Inspection Program made it difficult for the agencies to perform their duties to effectively protect U.S. agriculture from foreign pests and disease. For example, agency officials responsible for tracing prohibited agricultural items, had difficulty gaining access to ports for inspections in some instances because the agencies did not coordinate in advance. Even though the process for disseminating information is specified in an interagency agreement between DHS and USDA, the poor coordination made the specialists' assigned activities in the field difficult, if not impossible (GAO-06-644). According to agency officials, USDA and DHS have since taken steps to coordinate at ports of entry.

USDA Should Improve Coordination with Other Entities to Identify Research Gaps and Avoid Duplication

Applicable principles:
- Distinctiveness
- Effectiveness

The following key findings may contribute to the conversation on the 2012 Farm Bill concerning agricultural research programs:

- USDA does not have a documented, systematic process for tracking research conducted or under way that may fill the gaps identified in NPDRS recovery plans, which are intended to provide a brief primer on the plant disease discussed and identify research gaps and priorities, among other things. For example, the NPDRS recovery plan for stem rust on wheat—one of the most devastating plant diseases worldwide—states that current data on the disease must be reexamined and identifies 13 specific areas that require updated research. According to USDA officials, they rely on a variety of entities—including agencies within USDA, other federal agencies, state governments, land grant universities, and the private sector—to conduct research on plant diseases that could have high consequences for the agriculture sector. However, USDA does not have a systematic process for tracking research conducted or underway that may fill the gaps identified in the NPDRS recovery plans. Without a documented, systematic process to monitor the extent to which research gaps are filled, USDA may not have the critical information needed to help the nation recover from high-consequence plant diseases that could devastate the nation's production of economically important crops (GAO-11-652).

- DHS has the lead responsibility for coordinating research efforts to protect against agroterrorism but had no controls to coordinate efforts with other agencies such as USDA. For example, some of the DHS-supported activities, such as foreign animal disease research, appear to duplicate research conducted by USDA. Without the ability to track federally funded research efforts, the United States will not have a coordinated national approach to protect against agroterrorism, possibly resulting in gaps or needless duplication of effort (GAO-05-214). According to DHS, an interagency committee now ensures that research on foreign animal diseases is coordinated, but there is no similar effort for plants.

Section 8: Energy

In recent years, the federal government has increasingly encouraged the use of biofuels and other alternatives to petroleum in response to concerns over U.S. dependence on imported oil, climate change, and other issues. The U.S. transportation sector depends almost entirely on petroleum products refined from crude oil—primarily gasoline and diesel fuels—and the nation imports a significant portion of the crude oil and petroleum products consumed domestically.

The 2008 Farm Bill authorized a number of programs and tax provisions to encourage production, use, and development of biofuels, which can be an alternative to petroleum-based transportation fuels and are produced from renewable sources, primarily corn, sugar cane, and soybeans. Currently, the most commonly produced biofuel in the United States is ethanol, made primarily from corn. Corn is a relatively resource-intensive crop, requiring relatively higher rates of fertilizer and pesticide applications, and additional water to supplement rainfall, depending on where the crop is grown. Most U.S. corn is grown in the Midwest, and ethanol is generally produced near corn-producing areas.

Unlike petroleum products, which are primarily transported to wholesale terminals by pipelines, ethanol is transported to wholesale terminals by a combination of rail, tanker truck, and barge. At the terminals, most ethanol is blended with gasoline in mixtures generally containing up to 10 percent ethanol, E10. The blended fuel is transported by tanker truck to retail fueling outlets.

Congress has supported domestic ethanol production through tax incentives from the 1970s through 2011 and, more recently, through a renewable fuel standard (the fuel standard) that applies to transportation fuels used in the United States.[1] First enacted in 2005 and expanded in 2007, the fuel standard requires transportation fuels in the United States to contain certain volumes of biofuels, such as ethanol and biodiesel. The fuel standard generally requires the rising use of ethanol and other biofuels, from 9 billion gallons in 2008 to 36 billion gallons in 2022.

EPA is responsible for establishing and implementing regulations to ensure that the nation's transportation fuel supply contains the volumes of

---

[1]The Volumetric Ethanol Excise Tax Credit, which provided 45 cents per gallon to fuel blenders that purchased and blended ethanol with gasoline, expired on December 31, 2011.

biofuels required by the fuel standard. EPA recently allowed an intermediate blend, E15 (generally 15 percent ethanol), for use in model year 2001 and newer conventional automobiles, after determining that it would not cause these automobiles to be out of compliance with emissions standards.

The following are our key findings and applicable principles:

Increased Biofuels Production Has Agricultural and Environmental Effects

Applicable principle:
• Effectiveness

The following key findings may contribute to the conversation on the 2012 Farm Bill concerning the effects of producing biofuels:

• Increased production of ethanol (one type of biofuel) has raised demand for corn and contributed to higher corn prices, which has had several effects on U.S. agriculture. For example, with this demand, more acres have been planted to corn and fewer acres to other crops, and crop production has increased on lands that were formerly used for grazing or idled. Higher corn prices have created additional income for corn producers, but they have also driven up feed costs for livestock producers. The number of biorefineries has grown considerably, generally providing a boost to rural economies, although expert views vary on the magnitude and permanence of these benefits (GAO-09-446).

• Some experts believe that, because of the resources required, increased corn cultivation for ethanol production may contribute to additional water depletion and increased fertilizer and sediment runoff, impairing streams and other water bodies. Furthermore, as corn production increases, environmentally sensitive lands that are currently idled because they are enrolled in conservation programs may be moved back into production, thereby increasing cultivation of land that is susceptible to erosion and decreasing available habitat for wildlife, including threatened species. However, some of the effects on water quality and habitat may be mitigated by the use of agricultural conservation practices (GAO-09-446).

Investments in Fuel Delivery Infrastructure May Be Needed to Meet Mandated 2022 Ethanol Consumption Levels

Applicable principle:
  • Effectiveness

The following key findings may contribute to the conversation on the 2012 Farm Bill concerning challenges with building a biofuels infrastructure:

• Existing ethanol infrastructure should be sufficient to transport the nation's ethanol production through 2015 and meet fuel standard requirements, according to government and industry officials. Beyond 2015, however, large investments in infrastructure may be needed to transport enough ethanol to meet fuel standard requirements. According to EPA estimates, if an additional 9.4 billion gallons of ethanol are consumed domestically by 2022, several billion dollars would be needed to upgrade rail, truck, and barge infrastructure to transport ethanol to wholesale markets (GAO-11-513).

• EPA recently allowed an intermediate ethanol blend for use in certain automobiles, but several challenges and uncertainties must be addressed before intermediate blends can effectively help the nation meet fuel standard requirements and reduce dependence on petroleum imports. For example, key components of the nation's retail fueling infrastructure—such as gaskets and seals in dispensing equipment—could degrade or swell excessively and become ineffective when exposed to intermediate ethanol blends, and most existing equipment at retail fueling stations in the United States is not approved for use with intermediate blends (GAO-11-513).

Section 9: Crop Insurance and Disaster Assistance Programs

The cost of the federal crop insurance program—an average of about $7.3 billion annually from 2009 through 2011—has come under increased scrutiny because of the nation's severe budget constraints and because as crop prices have risen in recent years, so too has the value of the crops being insured, which results in higher crop insurance premiums and premium subsidies, as well as higher administrative cost reimbursements paid to crop insurance companies and their agents.

For decades, Congress has authorized a federal crop insurance program to help mitigate the financial risks inherent in farming—potential losses of crop production and revenue. To encourage participation in this program, USDA subsidizes farmers' insurance premiums, paying about 60 percent of the cost, and acts as the primary reinsurer for the private insurance companies that take on the risk of covering, or "underwriting," losses to insured farmers. These companies earn a profit (underwriting gains) when insurance premiums they collect exceed their payments to farmers for crop losses, and they incur underwriting losses if their payments to farmers for crop failures exceed the premiums. USDA also pays insurance companies an administrative allowance to cover the costs of selling and servicing policies. A standard reinsurance agreement between USDA and the companies establishes the terms and conditions under which the companies have to operate, including the rate for the companies' administrative allowance. Figure 3 shows the administrative allowances and underwriting gains or losses paid to crop insurance companies for 2000 through 2010.

**Figure 3: Administrative Allowances and Underwriting Gains or Losses Paid to
Crop Insurance Companies, 2000–2010**

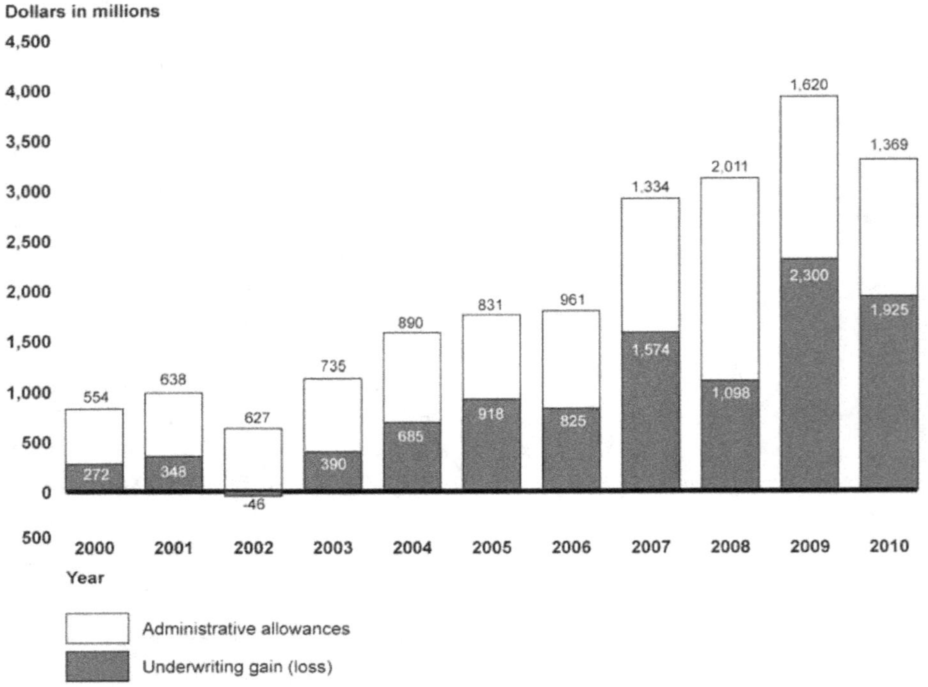

Dollars in millions

Year	Underwriting gain (loss)	Administrative allowances
2000	272	554
2001	348	638
2002	-46	627
2003	390	735
2004	685	890
2005	918	831
2006	825	961
2007	1,574	1,334
2008	1,098	2,011
2009	2,300	1,620
2010	1,925	1,369

Administrative allowances

Underwriting gain (loss)

Source: GAO analysis of USDA Risk Management Agency data.

To supplement the crop insurance program, Congress has historically
authorized ad hoc crop disaster assistance programs. These programs
generally provide one-time payments to compensate farmers for disaster-
related crop losses they sustain. The 2008 Farm Bill established and
funded a $3.8 billion- permanent trust fund for a new program—
Supplemental Revenue Assistance Payments (SURE) Program—to
provide disaster assistance to eligible farmers, but to qualify, farmers
must have lost crops on or before September 30, 2011.[1]

---

[1]The SURE program was authorized under the trade and tax provisions title (title XV) in
the 2008 Farm Bill, but we address it here because of its relevance to the crop insurance
and disaster assistance programs title (title XII).

The following are our key findings and applicable principles:

Limits on Crop Insurance Subsidies Would Save Money

Applicable principle:
- Affordability

The following key findings may contribute to the conversation on the 2012 Farm Bill concerning federal crop insurance subsidies:

- Crop insurance premium subsidies have more than doubled in recent years—from about $2.7 billion in 2006 to about $7.4 billion in 2011. Unlike many other farm programs, however, the crop insurance program has no limit on the amount of subsidy a farmer can receive. Other farm programs generally have statutory income and payment limits that apply to farmers. For example, a farmer with an average adjusted gross farm income (over the preceding 3 tax years) exceeding $750,000 is generally ineligible for direct payments, and farmers are subject to an annual limit of $40,000 per year on these payments. If, for example, the direct payment limit of $40,000 were applied to crop insurance subsidies to farmers for 2011, it would have saved up to $1 billion and would have affected less than 4 percent of farmers receiving the subsidies (GAO-12-256). In its comments, USDA said it was "ill-advised to reduce premium subsidies without further study. We disagreed and noted that the Administration included a reduction in premium subsidies in its proposed fiscal year 2013 budget.

USDA Has Reduced Costs by Decreasing Compensation to Insurance Companies, but Compensation May Still Be Excessive

Applicable principle:
- Affordability

The following key findings may contribute to the conversation on the 2012 Farm Bill concerning payments to crop insurance companies:

- In 2010, USDA paid crop insurance companies a total of about $1.9 billion in underwriting gains. In terms of profitability, these underwriting gains represent a rate of return of about 30 percent.[2] This rate of return exceeds USDA's target rate of return of 12 percent, which is based on a study of private insurance companies' rates of return (GAO-07-944T). The standard reinsurance agreement the federal government has with these companies beginning in 2011 reduces underwriting gains, but according to USDA, rates of return under the agreement are still expected to be higher than the agency's target.

---

[2]We calculated the 2010 rate of return using data on underwriting gains and retained premiums from USDA.

- From 2000 through 2009, USDA payments to insurance companies for administrative allowances nearly tripled—from $552 million in 2000 to an estimated $1.6 billion in 2009—according to our analysis of USDA data. This increase occurred primarily because the department's calculation method for administrative allowances considers crop prices, which rose dramatically, rather than crop insurance companies' actual expenses for selling and servicing policies, which generally remained stable (GAO-09-445). In response to our recommendation and consistent with provisions of the 2008 Farm Bill, in the 2011 standard reinsurance agreement, USDA capped administrative allowances, resulting in allowances that were lower than they otherwise would have been. In addition, in response to another one of our recommendations, USDA is taking steps to determine insurance agencies' reasonable costs for selling and servicing crop insurance policies.

USDA Has Strengthened Oversight of the Crop Insurance Program, but It Remains Vulnerable to Potential Fraud, Waste, and Abuse

Applicable principle:
- Oversight

The following key findings may contribute to the conversation on the 2012 Farm Bill concerning potential fraud, waste, and abuse in the federal crop insurance program:

- USDA employs a range of processes to help prevent and detect fraud, waste, and abuse in the crop insurance program, but it did not effectively use all the tools it had available in 2005 (GAO-05-528). Since 2005, USDA has improved its use of inspections, data analysis, oversight of insurance companies, and use of sanction authority. However, the department does not capitalize on all available data analysis tools to identify and prevent potential fraud, waste, and abuse, largely because of competing priorities.

- High premium subsidies, established by statute, may limit USDA's ability to control program abuse because the subsidies shield farmers from the full effect of paying higher premiums associated with frequent or larger claims (GAO-05-528 and GAO-07-944T). In March 2012, we suggested that Congress consider reducing premium subsidies (GAO-12-256).

Lessons Learned Could Improve Implementation of a Disaster Assistance Program

Applicable principle:
- Oversight

The following key findings may contribute to the conversation on the 2012 Farm Bill concerning federal disaster assistance programs:

- USDA's experience with the ad-hoc crop disaster programs from 2001 through 2007 shows that reviews to determine whether crop losses were eligible for payments occurred as many as 4 years after the crop losses primarily because of the time elapsed between when the disaster occurred and when an ad-hoc disaster assistance program was enacted. With such a lag, USDA county officials could not take actions, such as conducting field inspections, to validate whether the crops suffered damage as a result of a qualifying disaster. Many of the county officials said that having the opportunity to determine the eligibility of losses soon after the disaster would increase assurance that disaster program payments are proper (GAO-10-548). Timeliness of field inspections after crop losses is a continuing concern.

Appendix I: Scope and Methodology

To identify the universe of our evaluative reports issued since 2003 that are related to farm bill programs, we conducted searches in our internal and external databases, using calendar year 2003 as the starting point to include reports about programs implemented after passage of the 2002 Farm Bill—the Farm Security and Rural Investment Act of 2002. Our search went through July 31, 2011. For search terms, we used program names and legislation titles from the 2002 and 2008 farm bills, as well as U.S. Department of Agriculture agency names and farm bill titles from 1985 through 2008. Some of these search terms turned out to be over-inclusive, identifying numerous reports that were not related to farm bill programs. We filtered these results by adding search terms such as "farm" or "agriculture." For example, we took this step for the original search terms "disaster assistance" and "rural development." We eliminated certain types of products, such as reports on federal agency major rules (issued in compliance with the Congressional Review Act); legal decisions, opinions, and reports on bid protests, appropriations law, and other issues of federal law; and reports of survey results related to particular products. We also eliminated reports with no recommendations, because they generally did not address evaluative questions related to program integrity, effectiveness, or efficiency. In addition, we excluded testimonies based on reports already in the universe and reports we determined to be irrelevant to the farm bill. For example, our search terms yielded some reports focused entirely on wildfire management and food safety. In a few cases, we added reports that had not been identified through our database searches—for example, reports that were issued from August 1, 2011 through March 31, 2012. The final universe included 88 relevant reports.

To identify a list of principles significant to farm bill programs, we reviewed a subset of these reports—focusing on their findings and recommendations—and identified common themes related to program integrity, effectiveness, and efficiency. Using this list, we conducted a content analysis on the universe of reports, categorizing report text by principle and refining the principles as we did so. To ensure consistent interpretation and application of the principles, two analysts independently reviewed reports and reconciled any differences, until application of the principles was consistent between the two reviewers. We also reviewed some of our other products related to governmentwide issues and talked to experts on agricultural policy—such as a former Secretary of Agriculture, a former Member of Congress, other government officials, and an industry expert—to inform our final list of principles. We shared our list of principles with officials in the USDA Office of Inspector General, who adopted them for a companion report.

In addition, we summarized report findings related to 2008 Farm Bill titles where we had a significant body of work from 2003 through 2011 related to major provisions in the titles, and highlighted relevant principles where they applied. For those titles with a corresponding body of work, our reports and summaries do not cover all aspects of the farm bill title. For the research and related-matters title, we also included in our summary reports related to pertinent provisions under the miscellaneous title; and for the crop insurance and disaster assistance programs title, we also included in our summary a report related to a pertinent provision under the trade and tax provisions title. The 2008 Farm Bill titles without a corresponding body of our work since 2003 related to major provisions in the title include Title V (Credit), Title VIII (Forestry), Title X (Horticulture and Organic Agriculture), Title XI (Livestock), Title XIII (Commodity Futures), Title XIV (Miscellaneous), and Title XV (Trade and Tax Provisions).

We conducted our work from April 2011 through April 2012 in accordance with all sections of our *Quality Assurance Framework* that are relevant to our objectives. The framework requires that we plan and perform the engagement to obtain sufficient and appropriate evidence to meet our stated objectives and to discuss any limitations in our work. We believe that the information and data obtained, and the analysis conducted, provide a reasonable basis for any findings and conclusions in this product.

Appendix II: Related GAO Products, by 2008 Farm Bill Title

Reports covering material related to multiple farm bill titles are listed under each relevant title.

Title I: Commodity Programs

Follow-up on 2011 Report: Status of Actions Taken to Reduce Duplication, Overlap, and Fragmentation, Save Tax Dollars, and Enhance Revenue. GAO-12-453SP. Washington, D.C.: February 28, 2012.

U.S. Department of Agriculture: More Effective Management and Performance Can Help Implementation of the Farm Bill. GAO-11-779T. Washington, D.C.: June 23, 2011.

Opportunities to Reduce Potential Duplication in Government Programs, Save Tax Dollars, and Enhance Revenue. GAO-11-318SP. Washington, D.C.: March 1, 2011.

Federal Farm Programs: USDA Needs to Strengthen Controls to Prevent Payments to Individuals Who Exceed Income Eligibility Limits. GAO-09-67. Washington, D.C.: October 24, 2008.

Information Technology: Agriculture Needs to Strengthen Management Practices for Stabilizing and Modernizing Its Farm Program Delivery Systems. GAO-08-657. Washington, D.C.: May 16, 2008.

Beginning Farmers: Additional Steps Needed to Demonstrate the Effectiveness of USDA Assistance. GAO-07-1130. Washington, D.C.: September 18, 2007.

Federal Farm Programs: USDA Needs to Strengthen Controls to Prevent Improper Payments to Estates and Deceased Individuals. GAO-07-818. Washington, D.C.: July 9, 2007.

Suggested Areas for Oversight for the 110th Congress. GAO-07-235R. Washington, D.C.: November 17, 2006.

Tobacco Settlement: States' Allocations of Fiscal Year 2005 and Expected Fiscal Year 2006 Payments. GAO-06-502. Washington, D.C.: April 11, 2006.

Tobacco Settlement: States' Allocations of Fiscal Year 2004 and Expected Fiscal Year 2005 Payments. GAO-05-312. Washington, D.C.: March 21, 2005.

Dairy Industry: Information on Milk Prices, Factors Affecting Prices, and Dairy Policy Options. GAO-05-50. Washington, D.C.: December 29, 2004.

Farm Program Payments: USDA Needs to Strengthen Regulations and Oversight to Better Ensure Recipients Do Not Circumvent Payment Limitations. GAO-04-407. Washington, D.C.: April 30, 2004.

Tobacco Settlement: States' Allocations of Fiscal Year 2003 and Expected Fiscal Year 2004 Payments. GAO-04-518. Washington, D.C.: March 19, 2004.

Tobacco Settlement: States' Allocations of Fiscal Years 2002 and 2003 Master Settlement Agreement Payments. GAO-03-407. Washington, D.C.: February 28, 2003.

Title II: Conservation

Chesapeake Bay: Restoration Effort Needs Common Federal and State Goals and Assessment Approach. GAO-11-802. Washington, D.C.: September 15, 2011.

Recent Actions by the Chesapeake Bay Program Are Positive Steps Toward More Effectively Guiding the Restoration Effort, But Additional Steps Are Needed. GAO-08-1131R. Washington, D.C.: August 28, 2008.

Beginning Farmers: Additional Steps Needed to Demonstrate the Effectiveness of USDA Assistance. GAO-07-1130. Washington, D.C.: September 18, 2007.

US Fish and Wildlife Service: Additional Flexibility Needed to Deal with Farmlands Received from the Department of Agriculture. GAO-07-1092. Washington, D.C.: September 18, 2007.

Agricultural Conservation: Farm Program Payments Are an Important Factor in Landowners' Decisions to Convert Grassland to Cropland. GAO-07-1054. Washington, D.C.: September 10, 2007.

Agricultural Conservation: USDA Should Improve Its Management of Key Conservation Programs to Ensure Payments Promote Environmental Goals. GAO-07-370T. Washington, D.C.: January 17, 2007.

Suggested Areas for Oversight for the 110th Congress. GAO-07-235R. Washington, D.C.: November 17, 2006.

USDA Conservation Programs: Stakeholder Views on Participation and Coordination to Benefit Threatened and Endangered Species and Their Habitats. GAO-07-35. Washington, D.C.: November 15, 2006.

Agricultural Conservation: USDA Should Improve Its Process for Allocating Funds to States for the Environmental Quality Incentives Program. GAO-06-969. Washington, D.C.: September 22, 2006.

Conservation Security Program: Despite Cost Controls, Improved USDA Management Is Needed to Ensure Proper Payments and Reduce Duplication with Other Programs. GAO-06-312. Washington, D.C.: April 28, 2006.

Chesapeake Bay Program: Improved Strategies Are Needed to Better Assess, Report, and Manage Restoration Progress. GAO-06-96. Washington, D.C.: October 28, 2005.

Environmental Information: Status of Federal Data Programs That Support Ecological Indicators. GAO-05-376. Washington, D.C.: September 2, 2005.

Freshwater Programs: Federal Agencies' Funding in the United States and Abroad. GAO-05-253. Washington, D.C.: March 11, 2005.

Agricultural Conservation: USDA Should Improve Its Methods for Estimating Technical Assistance Costs. GAO-05-58. Washington, D.C.: November 30, 2004.

Agricultural Conservation: USDA Needs to Better Ensure Protection of Highly Erodible Cropland and Wetlands. GAO-03-418. Washington, D.C.: April 21, 2003.

Title III: Trade

International Food Assistance: Funding Development Projects through the Purchase, Shipment, and Sale of U.S. Commodities Is Inefficient and Can Cause Adverse Market Impacts. GAO-11-636. Washington, D.C.: June 23, 2011.

International School Feeding: USDA's Oversight of the McGovern-Dole Food for Education Program Needs Improvement. GAO-11-544. Washington, D.C.: May 19, 2011.

International Food Assistance: Better Nutrition and Quality Control Can Further Improve U.S. Food Aid. GAO-11-491. Washington, D.C.: May 12, 2011.

International Trade: Exporters' Use of the Earned Import Allowance Program for Haiti is Negligible because They Favor Other Trade Provisions. GAO-10-654. Washington, D.C.: June 16, 2010.

Global Food Security: U.S. Agencies Progressing on Governmentwide Strategy, but Approach Faces Several Vulnerabilities. GAO-10-352. Washington, D.C.: March 11, 2010.

Softwood Lumber Act of 2008: Customs and Border Protection Established Required Procedures, but Agencies Report Little Benefit from New Requirements. GAO-10-220. Washington, D.C.: December 18, 2009.

International Food Assistance: Key Issues for Congressional Oversight. GAO-09-977SP. Washington, D.C.: September 30, 2009.

International Food Assistance: USAID Is Taking Actions to Improve Monitoring and Evaluation of Nonemergency Food Aid, but Weaknesses in Planning Could Impede Efforts. GAO-09-980. Washington, D.C.: September 28, 2009.

U.S. and Canadian Governments Have Established Mechanisms to Monitor Compliance with the 2006 Softwood Lumber Agreement but Face Operational Challenges. GAO-09-764R. Washington, D.C.: June 18, 2009.

International Food Assistance: Local and Regional Procurement Can Enhance the Efficiency of U.S. Food Aid, but Challenges May Constrain Its Implementation. GAO-09-570. Washington, D.C.: May 29, 2009.

International Food Security: Insufficient Efforts by Host Governments and Donors Threaten Progress to Halve Hunger in Sub-Saharan Africa by 2015. GAO-08-680. Washington, D.C.: May 29, 2008.

Foreign Assistance: Various Challenges Impede the Efficiency and Effectiveness of U.S. Food Aid. GAO-07-560. Washington, D.C.: April 13, 2007.

Title IV: Nutrition

Follow-up on 2011 Report: Status of Actions Taken to Reduce Duplication, Overlap, and Fragmentation, Save Tax Dollars, and Enhance Revenue. GAO-12-453SP. Washington, D.C.: February 28, 2012.

U.S. Department of Agriculture: More Effective Management and Performance Can Help Implementation of the Farm Bill. GAO-11-779T. Washington, D.C.: June 23, 2011.

School Meal Programs: More Systematic Development of Specifications Could Improve the Safety of Foods Purchased through USDA's Commodity Program. GAO-11-376. Washington, D.C.: May 3, 2011.

Opportunities to Reduce Potential Duplication in Government Programs, Save Tax Dollars, and Enhance Revenue. GAO-11-318SP. Washington, D.C.: March 1, 2011.

Supplemental Nutrition Assistance Program: Payment Errors and Trafficking Have Declined, but Challenges Remain. GAO-10-956T. Washington, D.C.: July 28, 2010.

Domestic Food Assistance: Complex System Benefits Millions, but Additional Efforts Could Address Potential Inefficiency and Overlap among Smaller Programs. GAO-10-346. Washington, D.C.: April 15, 2010.

School Meal Programs: Improved Reviews, Federal Guidance, and Data Collection Needed to Address Counting and Claiming Errors. GAO-09-814. Washington, D.C.: September 9, 2009.

School Meal Programs: Changes to Federal Agencies' Procedures Could Reduce Risk of School Children Consuming Recalled Food. GAO-09-649. Washington, D.C.: August 20, 2009.

School Meal Programs: Experiences of the States and Districts that Eliminated Reduced-price Fees. GAO-09-584. Washington, D.C.: July 17, 2009.

Sponsored Noncitizens and Public Benefits: More Clarity in Federal Guidance and Better Access to Federal Information Could Improve Implementation of Income Eligibility Rules. GAO-09-375. Washington, D.C.: May 19, 2009.

Meal Counting and Claiming by Food Service Management Companies in the School Meal Programs. GAO-09-156R. Washington, D.C.: January 30, 2009.

Food Stamp Program: Options for Delivering Financial Incentives to Participants for Purchasing Targeted Foods. GAO-08-415. Washington, D.C.: July 30, 2008.

Food Stamp Program: Use of Alternative Methods to Apply for and Maintain Benefits Could Be Enhanced by Additional Evaluation and Information on Promising Practices. GAO-07-573. Washington, D.C.: May 3, 2007.

Food Stamp Program: FNS Could Improve Guidance and Monitoring to Help Ensure Appropriate Use of Noncash Categorical Eligibility. GAO-07-465. Washington, D.C.: March 28, 2007.

Food Stamp Trafficking: FNS Could Enhance Program Integrity by Better Targeting Stores Likely to Traffic and Increasing Penalties. GAO-07-53. Washington, D.C.: October 13, 2006.

WIC Program: More Detailed Price and Quantity Data Could Enhance Agriculture's Assessment of WIC Program Expenditures. GAO-06-664. Washington, D.C.: July 28, 2006.

Food Assistance: FNS Could Take Additional Steps to Contain WIC Infant Formula Costs. GAO-06-380. Washington, D.C.: March 28, 2006.

Breastfeeding: Some Strategies Used to Market Infant Formula May Discourage Breastfeeding; State Contracts Should Better Protect Against Misuse of WIC Name. GAO-06-282. Washington, D.C.: February 8, 2006.

School Meal Programs: Competitive Foods Are Widely Available and Generate Substantial Revenues for Schools. GAO-05-563. Washington, D.C.: August 8, 2005.

Food Stamp Program: States Have Made Progress Reducing Payment Errors, and Further Challenges Remain. GAO-05-245. Washington, D.C.: May 5, 2005.

Food Stamp Program: Farm Bill Options Ease Administrative Burden, but Opportunities Exist to Streamline Participant Reporting Rules among Programs. GAO-04-916. Washington, D.C.: September 16, 2004.

Nutrition Education: USDA Provides Services through Multiple Programs, but Stronger Linkages among Efforts Are Needed. GAO-04-528. Washington, D.C.: April 27, 2004.

School Meal Programs: Competitive Foods Are Available in Many Schools; Actions Taken to Restrict Them Differ by State and Locality. GAO-04-673. Washington, D.C.: April 23, 2004.

Food Stamp Program: Steps Have Been Taken to Increase Participation of Working Families, but Better Tracking of Efforts Is Needed. GAO-04-346. Washington, D.C.: March 5, 2004.

Opportunities for Oversight and Improved Use of Taxpayer Funds; Examples from Selected GAO Work. GAO-03-1006. Washington, D.C.: August 1, 2003.

School Meal Programs: Few Instances of Foodborne Outbreaks Reported, but Opportunities Exist to Enhance Outbreak Data and Food Safety Practices. GAO-03-530. Washington, D.C.: May 9, 2003.

School Meal Programs: Revenue and Expense Information from Selected States. GAO-03-569. Washington, D.C.: May 9, 2003.

School Lunch Program: Efforts Needed to Improve Nutrition and Encourage Healthy Eating. GAO-03-506. Washington, D.C.: May 9, 2003.

Food Stamp Employment and Training Program: Better Data Needed to Understand Who Is Served and What the Program Achieves. GAO-03-388. Washington, D.C.: March 12, 2003.

Food Assistance: Potential to Serve More WIC Infants by Reducing Formula Cost. GAO-03-331. Washington, D.C.: February 12, 2003.

Title V: Credit

Beginning Farmers: Additional Steps Needed to Demonstrate the Effectiveness of USDA Assistance. GAO-07-1130. Washington, D.C.: September 18, 2007.

Farm Loan Programs: GAO Reports on USDA Lending Practices. GAO-06-912R. Washington, D.C.: June 28, 2006.

| Title VI: Rural Development | *2012 Annual Report: Opportunities to Reduce Duplication, Overlap and Fragmentation, Achieve Savings, and Enhance Revenue.* GAO-12-342SP. Washington, D.C.: February 28, 2012. |

2012 Annual Report: Opportunities to Reduce Duplication, Overlap and Fragmentation, Achieve Savings, and Enhance Revenue. GAO-12-342SP. Washington, D.C.: February 28, 2012.

Follow-up on 2011 Report: Status of Actions Taken to Reduce Duplication, Overlap, and Fragmentation, Save Tax Dollars, and Enhance Revenue. GAO-12-453SP. Washington, D.C.: February 28, 2012.

U.S. Department of Agriculture: More Effective Management and Performance Can Help Implementation of the Farm Bill. GAO-11-779T. Washington, D.C.: June 23, 2011.

Efficiency and Effectiveness of Fragmented Economic Development Programs Are Unclear. GAO-11-477R. Washington, D.C.: May 19, 2011.

Department of Agriculture, Rural Utilities Service: Rural Broadband Access Loans and Loan Guarantees. GAO-11-541R. Washington, D.C.: April 7, 2011.

Opportunities to Reduce Potential Duplication in Government Programs, Save Tax Dollars, and Enhance Revenue. GAO-11-318SP. Washington, D.C.: March 1, 2011.

The Housing Assistance Council's Use of Appropriated Funds. GAO-11-189R. Washington, D.C.: December 6, 2010.

Rural Water Infrastructure: Improved Coordination and Funding Processes Could Enhance Federal Efforts to meet Needs in the U.S.-Mexico Border Region. GAO-10-126. Washington, D.C.: December 18, 2009.

Telecommunications: Broadband Deployment Plan Should Include Performance Goals and Measures to Guide Federal Investment. GAO-09-494. Washington, D.C.: May 12, 2009.

Rural Economic Development: Collaboration between SBA and USDA Could Be Improved. GAO-08-1123. Washington, D.C.: September 18, 2008.

Federal Electricity Subsidies: Information on Research Funding, Tax Expenditures, and Other Activities That Support Electricity Production. GAO-08-102. Washington, D.C.: October 26, 2007.

Water Resources: Four Federal Agencies Provide Funding for Rural Water Supply and Wastewater Projects. GAO-07-1094. Washington, D.C.: September 7, 2007.

Telecommunications: Broadband Deployment Is Extensive throughout the United States, but It Is Difficult to Assess the Extent of Deployment Gaps in Rural Areas. GAO-06-426. Washington, D.C.: May 5, 2006.

Rural Economic Development: More Assurance Is Needed That Grant Funding Information Is Accurately Reported. GAO-06-294. Washington, D.C.: February 24, 2006.

Rural Housing Service: Overview of Program Issues. GAO-05-382T. Washington, D.C.: March 10, 2005.

Information Resource Management Internal Control Issues. GAO-05-288R. Washington, D.C.: March 10, 2005.

Rural Housing: Changing the Definition of Rural Could Improve Eligibility Determinations. GAO-05-110. Washington, D.C.: December 3, 2004.

Rural Utilities Service: Opportunities to Better Target Assistance to Rural Areas and Avoid Unnecessary Financial Risk. GAO-04-647. Washington, D.C.: June 18, 2004.

Rural Housing Service: Opportunities to Improve Management. GAO-03-911T. Washington, D.C.: June 19, 2003.

Title VII: Research and Related Matters

2012 Annual Report: Opportunities to Reduce Duplication, Overlap and Fragmentation, Achieve Savings, and Enhance Revenue. GAO-12-342SP. Washington, D.C.: February 28, 2012.

Follow-up on 2011 Report: Status of Actions Taken to Reduce Duplication, Overlap, and Fragmentation, Save Tax Dollars, and Enhance Revenue. GAO-12-453SP. Washington, D.C.: February 28, 2012.

Antibiotic Resistance: Agencies Have Made Limited Progress Addressing Antibiotic Use in Animals. GAO-11-801. Washington, D.C.: September 7, 2011.

Homeland Security: Actions Needed to Improve Response to Potential Terrorist Attacks and Natural Disasters Affecting Food and Agriculture. GAO-11-652. Washington, D.C.: August 19, 2011.

Opportunities to Reduce Potential Duplication in Government Programs, Save Tax Dollars, and Enhance Revenue. GAO-11-318SP. Washington, D.C.: March 1, 2011.

Live Animal Imports: Agencies Need Better Collaboration to Reduce the Risk of Animal-Related Diseases. GAO-11-9. Washington, D.C.: November 8, 2010.

Biosurveillance: Efforts to Develop a National Biosurveillance Capability Need a National Strategy and a Designated Leader. GAO-10-645. Washington, D.C.: June 30, 2010.

Biological Research: Observations on DHS's Analyses Concerning Whether FMD Research Can Be Done as Safely on the Mainland as on Plum Island. GAO-09-747. Washington, D.C.: July 30, 2009.

Genetically Engineered Crops: Agencies Are Proposing Changes to Improve Oversight, but Could Take Additional Steps to Enhance Coordination and Monitoring. GAO-09-60. Washington, D.C.: December 5, 2008.

Agricultural Quarantine Inspection Program: Management Problems May Increase Vulnerability of U.S. Agriculture to Foreign Pests and Diseases. GAO-08-96T. Washington, D.C.: October 3, 2007.

Plum Island Animal Disease Center: DHS Has Made Significant Progress Implementing Security Recommendations, but Several Recommendations Remain Open. GAO-08-306R. Washington, D.C.: December 17, 2007.

Avian Influenza: USDA Has Taken Important Steps to Prepare for Outbreaks, but Better Planning Could Improve Response. GAO-07-652. Washington, D.C.: June 11, 2007.

USDA: Information on Classical Plant and Animal Breeding Activities. GAO-07-1171R. Washington, D.C.: September 13, 2007.

Homeland Security: Management and Coordination Problems Increase the Vulnerability of U.S. Agriculture to Foreign Pests and Disease. GAO-06-644. Washington, D.C.: May 19, 2006.

Agriculture Production: USDA Needs to Build on 2005 Experience to Minimize the Effects of Asian Soybean Rust in the Future. GAO-06-337. Washington, D.C.: February 24, 2006.

Plum Island Animal Disease Center: DHS and USDA Are Successfully Coordinating Current Work, but Long-Term Plans Are Being Assessed. GAO-06-132. Washington, D.C.: December 19, 2005.

Agriculture Production: USDA's Preparation for Asian Soybean Rust. GAO-05-668R. Washington, D.C.: May 17, 2005.

Homeland Security: Much Is Being Done to Protect Agriculture from a Terrorist Attack, but Important Challenges Remain. GAO-05-214. Washington, D.C.: March 8, 2005.

Combating Bioterrorism: Actions Needed to Improve Security at Plum Island Animal Disease Center. GAO-03-847. Washington, D.C.: September 19, 2003.

Title VIII: Forestry	*U.S. Department of Agriculture: More Effective Management and Performance Can Help Implementation of the Farm Bill.* GAO-11-779T. Washington, D.C.: June 23, 2011.
	Forest Service Research and Development: Improvements in Delivery of Research Results Can Help Ensure That Benefits of Research Are Realized. GAO-11-12. Washington, D.C.: October 29, 2010.
Title IX: Energy	*Follow-up on 2011 Report: Status of Actions Taken to Reduce Duplication, Overlap, and Fragmentation, Save Tax Dollars, and Enhance Revenue.* GAO-12-453SP. Washington, D.C.: February 28, 2012.
	Biofuels: Challenges to the Transportation, Sale, and Use of Intermediate Ethanol Blends. GAO-11-513. Washington, D.C.: June 3, 2011.
	Opportunities to Reduce Potential Duplication in Government Programs, Save Tax Dollars, and Enhance Revenue. GAO-11-318SP. Washington, D.C.: March 1, 2011.

Biofuels: Potential Effects and Challenges of Required Increases in Production and Use. GAO-09-446. Washington, D.C.: August 25, 2009.

Biofuels: DOE Lacks a Strategic Approach to Coordinate Increasing Production with Infrastructure Development and Vehicle Needs. GAO-07-713. Washington, D.C.: June 8, 2007.

Wood Utilization: Federal Research and Product Development Activities, Support, and Technology Transfer. GAO-06-624. Washington, D.C.: June 15, 2006.

Natural Resources: Woody Biomass Users' Experiences Offer Insights for Government Efforts Aimed at Promoting Its Use. GAO-06-336. Washington, D.C.: March 22, 2006.

Natural Resources: Federal Agencies Are Engaged in Various Efforts to Promote the Utilization of Woody Biomass, but Significant Obstacles to Its Use Remain. GAO-05-373. Washington, D.C.: May 13, 2005.

Renewable Energy: Wind Power's Contribution to Electric Power Generation and Impact on Farms and Rural Communities. GAO-04-756. Washington, D.C.: September 3, 2004.

Biobased Products: Improved USDA Management Would Help Agencies Comply with Farm Bill Purchasing Requirements. GAO-04-437. Washington, D.C.: April 7, 2004.

Title X: Horticulture and Organic Agriculture	No GAO reports meeting our selection criteria were issued between 2003 and March 2012 related to this title.
Title XI: Livestock	*U.S. Department of Agriculture: More Effective Management and Performance Can Help Implementation of the Farm Bill.* GAO-11-779T. Washington, D.C.: June 23, 2011. *Horse Welfare: Action Needed to Address Unintended Consequences from Cessation of Domestic Slaughter.* GAO-11-228. Washington, D.C.: June 22, 2011. *Live Animal Imports: Agencies Need Better Collaboration to Reduce the Risk of Animal-Related Diseases.* GAO-11-9. Washington, D.C.: November 8, 2010.

Animal Welfare: USDA's Oversight of Dealers of Random Source Dogs and Cats Would Benefit from Additional Management Information and Analysis. GAO-10-945. Washington, D.C.: September 24, 2010.

Humane Methods of Slaughter Act: Actions Are Needed to Strengthen Enforcement. GAO-10-203. Washington, D.C.: February 19, 2010.

Veterinarian Workforce: Actions Are Needed to Ensure Sufficient Capacity for Protecting Public and Animal Health. GAO-09-178. Washington, D.C.: February 4, 2009.

Humane Methods of Handling and Slaughter: Public Reporting on Violations Can Identify Enforcement Challenges and Enhance Transparency. GAO-08-686T. Washington, D.C.: April 17, 2008.

Humane Methods of Slaughter Act: USDA Has Addressed Some Problems but Still Faces Enforcement Challenges. GAO-04-247. Washington, D.C.: January 30, 2004.

Country-of-Origin Labeling: Opportunities for USDA and Industry to Implement Challenging Aspects of the New Law. GAO-03-780. Washington, D.C.: August 5, 2003.

Title XII: Crop Insurance and Disaster Assistance Programs	*Crop Insurance: Savings Would Result from Program Changes and Greater Use of Data Mining.* GAO-12-256. Washington, D.C.: March 13, 2012.

U.S. Department of Agriculture: More Effective Management and Performance Can Help Implementation of the Farm Bill. GAO-11-779T. Washington, D.C.: June 23, 2011.

USDA Crop Disaster Programs: Lessons Learned Can Improve Implementation of New Crop Assistance Program. GAO-10-548. Washington, D.C.: June 4, 2010.

Small Business Administration: Continued Attention Needed to Address Reforms to the Disaster Loan Program. GAO-10-735T. Washington, D.C.: May 19, 2010.

Crop Insurance: Opportunities Exist to Reduce the Costs of Administering the Program. GAO-09-445. Washington, D.C.: April 29, 2009.

Beginning Farmers: Additional Steps Needed to Demonstrate the Effectiveness of USDA Assistance. GAO-07-1130. Washington, D.C.: September 18, 2007.

Crop Insurance: Continuing Efforts Are Needed to Improve Program Integrity and Ensure Program Costs Are Reasonable. GAO-07-944T. Washington, D.C.: June 7, 2007.

Suggested Areas for Oversight for the 110th Congress. GAO-07-235R. Washington, D.C.: November 17, 2006.

Crop Insurance: Actions Needed to Reduce Program's Vulnerability to Fraud, Waste, and Abuse. GAO-05-528. Washington, D.C.: September 30, 2005.

Crop Insurance: USDA Needs to Improve Oversight of Insurance Companies and Develop a Policy to Address Any Future Insolvencies. GAO-04-517. Washington, D.C.: June 1, 2004.

Title XIII: Commodity Futures	*Commodity Futures Trading Commission: Trends in Energy Derivatives Markets Raise Questions about CFTC's Oversight.* GAO-08-25. Washington, D.C.: October 19, 2007.
Title XIV: Miscellaneous	*U.S. Department of Agriculture: More Effective Management and Performance Can Help Implementation of the Farm Bill.* GAO-11-779T. Washington, D.C.: June 23, 2011.
	US Department of Agriculture: Recommendations and Options to Address Management Deficiencies in the Office of the Assistant Secretary for Civil Rights. GAO-09-62. Washington, D.C.: October 22, 2008.
Title XV: Trade and Tax Provisions	No GAO reports meeting our selection criteria were issued between 2003 and March 2012 related to this title.

Appendix III: Related USDA Office of Inspector General Products, by 2008 Farm Bill Title

Title I: Commodity Programs

Calendar Year 2010 Executive Order 13520, Reducing Improper Payments, High Dollar Report Review. 50024-0001-FM. Washington, D.C.: July 15, 2011.[1]

Fiscal Year 2010 Farm Service Agency Farm Assistance Program Payments. 03024-0001-11. Washington, D.C.: June 21, 2011.

Agreed-Upon Procedures – Farm Service Agency Average Crop Revenue Election Program, Sheridan County, Montana. 03099-0199-KC. Washington, D.C.: December 10, 2010.

Farm Service Agency's Reliance on the National Agricultural Statistics Service's Published Peanut Prices. 50601-0014-KC. Washington, D.C.: March, 31, 2009.

Farm Service Agency: Payment Limitation Attestation Review in Wharton County, Texas. 03099-0182-Te. Washington, D.C.: October 23, 2008.

Methodology for Establishing National/Regional Loan Rates for USDA's Pulse Crop Loan Program. 03601-0026-KC. Washington, D.C.: September 25, 2008.

Farm Service Agency: Payment Limitation Review in Louisiana. 03099-0181-Te. Washington, D.C.: May 8, 2008.

Identification and Reporting of Improper Payments in FSA High Risk Programs. 03601-0016-Ch. Washington, D.C.: March 27, 2008.

Improper Payments: Monitoring the Progress of Corrective Actions for High-Risk Programs in the Farm Service Agency. 03601-0014-Ch. Washington, D.C.: May 18, 2007.

Farm Service Agency: Efforts to Identify and Recover Overpayments in the Direct and Counter-Cyclical Program. 03008-0001-At. Washington, D.C.: December 12, 2006.

Farm Service Agency: Disposition of Nonfat Dry Milk. 03099-0197-KC. Washington, D.C.: September 20, 2006.

---

[1]Other agencies and provisions are also included in this audit.

Farm Service Agency: Nonrecourse Marketing Assistance Farm-Stored Loans. 03601-0047-Te. Washington, D.C.: September 13, 2006.

Farm Service Agency: Direct and Counter-Cyclical Program. 03099-0196-KC. Washington, D.C.: April 24, 2006

Farm Service Agency: Tracking Finality Rule and Equitable Relief Decisions. 03601-0044-Te. Washington, D.C.: March 27, 2006.

Farm Service Agency's Progress To Implement the Improper Payments Information Act of 2002. 03601-0013-Ch. Washington, D.C.: March 6, 2006.

Farm Service Agency: Compliance Activities. 03601-0012-Ch. Washington, D.C.: September 30, 2005.

Farm Service Agency: Compliance with the Improper Payments Information Act of 2002. 03601-0046-Te. Washington, D.C.: March 21, 2005.

USDA Compliance with the Improper Payments Information Act of 2002. 50601-0008-Ch. Washington, D.C.: January 11, 2005.[2]

Farm Service Agency: Milk Income Loss Contract (MILC) Program. 03601-0010-Ch. Washington, D.C.: December 21, 2004.

Farm Service Agency: Farm Programs Audit in a Louisiana Parish. 03601-0042-Te. Temple, TX: March 19, 2004.

Farm Service Agency: Review of the 2002 Farm Bill Commodity Loan and Payment Rates. 03601-0020-KC. Washington, D.C.: December 22, 2003.

---

[2]Other agencies and provisions are also included in this audit.

Title II: Conservation	*Controls Over the Farm and Ranch Lands Protection Program in Michigan.* 10099-0003-Ch. Washington, D.C.: September 14, 2011.

Natural Resources Conservation Service: Farm and Ranch Lands Protection Program Review of Non-Governmental Organizations. 10099-0006-SF. Washington, D.C.: July 6, 2009.

Natural Resources Conservation Service: Conservation Security Program. 10601-0004-KC. Washington, D.C.: June 25, 2009.

Farm Service Agency: Hurricane Relief Initiatives: Emergency Forestry Conservation Reserve Program. 03601-0024-KC. Washington, D.C.: September 17, 2008

Natural Resources Conservation Service: Wetlands Reserve Program Wetlands Restoration and Compliance. 10099-0004-SF. Washington, D.C.: August 25, 2008.

Natural Resources Conservation Service: Status Review Process. 50601-0013-KC. Washington, D.C.: June 11, 2008.

Natural Resources Conservation Service and Farm Service Agency: Crop Bases on Lands With Conservation Easements in California. 50099-0011-SF. Washington, D.C.: August 27, 2007.

Evaluation Report: Saving the Chesapeake Bay Watershed Requires Better Coordination of Environmental and Agricultural Resources. 50601-0010-HQ. Washington, D.C.: November 20, 2006.

Natural Resources Conservation Service: Farm and Ranch Lands Protection Program in Alabama. 10099-0005-SF. Washington, D.C.: September 5, 2006.

Improper Payments – Monitoring the Progress of Corrective Actions for High Risk Programs in Natural Resources Conservation Service. 10601-0003-Ch. Washington, D.C.: June 12, 2006.

Natural Resources Conservation Service: Wetlands Reserve Program Compensation for Easements Washington, D.C. 10099-0003-SF. Washington, D.C.: August 8, 2005.

*Natural Resources Conservation Service: Environmental Quality
Incentives Program.* 10099-0018-KC. Washington, D.C.:
February 28, 2005.

*Natural Resources Conservation Service: Compliance with the Improper
Payments Information Act of 2002.* 10601-0003-KC. Washington, D.C.:
January 10, 2005.

Title III: Trade

*USDA's Role in the Export of Genetically Engineered Agricultural
Commodities.* 50601-0014-Te. Washington, D.C.: February 20, 2009.[3]

*Farm Service Agency: Inspection of Temporary Domestic Storage Sites
for Foreign Food Assistance.* 03099-0198-KC. Washington, D.C.:
August 22, 2008.

Export Credit Guarantee Program. 07601-0002-Hy. Washington, D.C.:
July 22, 2008.

Foreign Agricultural Service: Implementation of the Trade Title of the
2002 Farm Bill and the President's Management Agenda. 50601-0012-At.
Washington, D.C.: March 28, 2007.

Foreign Agricultural Service: Trade Promotion Operations. 07601-0001-Hy.
Washington, D.C.: February 22, 2007.

*Foreign Agricultural Service: Private Voluntary Organization Grant Fund
Accountability.* 07016-0001-At. Washington, D.C.: March 15, 2006.

*Farm Service Agency: Analysis of Farm Service Agency/Commodity
Credit Corporation Wheat Sales.* 03801-0006-KC. Washington, D.C.:
September 30, 2004.

---

[3]Report also discuses information contained under Title VII- Research and Related
Matters.

Title IV: Nutrition

*Identifying Areas of Risk in the Child and Adult Care Food Program
(CACFP) Using Automated Data Analysis Tools.* 27099-0001-DA.
Washington, D.C.: January 31, 2012.

*Analysis of Louisiana's Supplemental Nutrition Assistance Program
(SNAP) Eligibility Data.* 27002-0003-13. Washington, D.C.:
January 31, 2012.

*Analysis of Alabama's Supplemental Nutrition Assistance Program
(SNAP) Eligibility Data.* 27002-0004-13. Washington, D.C.:
January 31, 2012.

*Analysis of Mississippi's Supplemental Nutrition Assistance Program
(SNAP) Eligibility Data.* 27002-0005-13. Washington, D.C.:
January 31, 2012.

*State Fraud Detection Efforts for the Supplemental Nutrition Assistance
Program.* 27703-0002-Hy. Washington, D.C.: January 27, 2012.

*Analysis of Florida's Supplemental Nutrition Assistance Program (SNAP)
Eligibility Data.* 27002-0002-13. Washington, D.C.: November 29, 2011.

*Analysis of Kansas' Supplemental Nutrition Assistance Program (SNAP)
Eligibility Data.* 27002-0001-13. Washington, D.C.: November 23, 2011.

*Analysis of Supplemental Nutrition Assistance Program (SNAP) Anti-
Fraud Locator EBT Retailer Transactions (ALERT) Database.*
27002-0001-DA. Washington, D.C.: November 22, 2011.

Controls over Outsourcing of Food and Nutrition Service's Supplemental
Nutrition Assistance Program Electronic Benefits Transfer Call Centers.
27703-0001-Te. Washington, D.C.: June 30, 2011.

*Calendar Year 2010 Executive Order 13520, Reducing Improper
Payments, Accountable Official Report Review.* 50024-0002-FM.
Washington, D.C.: March 23, 2011.

Recovery Act Equipment and Facility Assistance – Food and Nutrition
Service's Food Distribution Program on Indian Reservations Phase I.
27703-0002-HQ. Washington, D.C.: September 30, 2010.

Oversight of the Recovery Act WIC Contingency Funds. 27703-0001-Ch.
Washington, D.C.: April 22, 2010.

*Followup on the Agricultural Marketing Service's Purchases of Frozen
Ground Beef.* 01601-0002-Hy. Washington, D.C.: April 12, 2010.

Review of the Emergency Food Assistance Program. 27703-0001-At.
Washington, D.C.: March 31, 2010.

Summary of Nationwide Electronic Benefits Transfer Operations.
27099-0071-Hy. Washington, D.C.: January 26, 2010.

Funds Provided by the American Recovery and Reinvestment Act for
Management and Oversight of the Supplemental Nutrition Assistance
Program. 27703-0001-Hy. Washington, D.C.: December 16, 2009.

*Supplemental Nutrition Assistance Program Benefits and the Thrifty Food
Plan.* 27703-0001-KC. Washington, D.C.: December 3, 2009.

*Follow-up on FNS Disaster Supplemental Nutrition Assistance Program
for Hurricanes Katrina and Rita.* 27601-0011-Te. Washington, D.C.:
June 2, 2009.

Monitoring of CACFP Sponsor, Collaborative Network, Toledo, Ohio.
27601-0037-Ch. Chicago, IL: February 26, 2009.

Food and Nutrition Service's Continued Monitoring of EBT Operations –
State of California Department of Social Services. 27099-0035-SF. San
Francisco, CA: December 4, 2008.

Food Stamp Program Retailer Authorization and Store Visits.
27601-0015-At. Washington, D.C.: September 26, 2008.

*Food and Nutrition Service: Food Stamp Program, Administrative Costs
New Jersey.* 27002-0025-Hy. Beltsville, MD: September 10, 2008.

Electronic Benefits Transfer System State of Colorado. 27099-0068-Hy.
Beltsville, MD: June 20, 2008.

*Food and Nutrition Service: Summer Food Service Program Operated by
the State of Georgia.* 27099-0063-At. Beltsville, MD: March 31, 2008.

Food Stamp Employment and Training Program. 27601-0016-At.
Washington, D.C.: March 31, 2008.

Food and Nutrition Service: JPMorgan EFS' Oversight of EBT Operations. 27099-0069-Hy. Washington, D.C.: September 28, 2007.

Food and Nutrition Service: Disaster Food Stamp Program for Hurricanes Katrina and Rita – Louisiana, Mississippi, and Texas. 27099-0049-Te. Washington, D.C.: September 4, 2007.

Food and Nutrition Service: Western Region Summer Food Service Program California and Nevada. 27099-0034-SF. San Francisco, CA: August 17, 2007.

Special Supplemental Nutrition Program for Women, Infants, and Children, Puerto Rico. 27004-0004-At. Atlanta, GA: May 24, 2007.

Meal Accountability at Choice Schools in Milwaukee, Wisconsin. 27004-0005-Ch. Chicago, IL: May 3, 2007.

Food and Nutrition Service: National Office Oversight of Electronic Benefits Transfer Operations. 27099-0066-Hy. Washington, D.C.: September 28, 2006.

Food and Nutrition Service: Child Nutrition Labeling Program. 27601-0013-Hy. Washington, D.C.: September 28, 2006.

Food and Nutrition Service: Disaster Food Stamp Program for Hurricanes Katrina, Rita, and Wilma – Alabama and Florida. 27099-0061-At. Atlanta, GA: August 30, 2006.

Food and Nutrition Service: Food Stamp Program, ALERT Watch List. 27099-0032-SF. Washington, D.C.: July 28, 2006.

Child and Adult Care Food Program: Supper Meals Served in Schools. 27601-0035-Ch. Washington, D.C.: July 14, 2006.

WIC Administrative Costs in Georgia. 27002-0002-At. Atlanta, GA: March 31, 2006.

*USDA's Progress to Implement the Improper Payments Information Act of
2002.* 50601-0010-Ch. Washington, D.C.: February 13, 2006.[4]

*Food and Nutrition Service: Special Wages Incentive Program in Puerto
Rico.* 27099-0060-At. Atlanta, GA: December 23, 2005.

Food and Nutrition Service: National School Lunch Program: Cost-
Reimbursable Contracts with a Food Service Management Company.
27601-0015-KC. Washington, D.C.: December 9, 2005.

*Audit of the Avella, PA School District's Use of National School Lunch
Program Funds.* 27010-0034-Hy. Beltsville, MD: December 1, 2005.

Food and Nutrition Service: Special Supplemental Nutrition Program For
Women, Infants, and Children, Administrative Costs – Oregon.
27099-0033-SF. San Francisco, CA: November 16, 2005.

*Agricultural Marketing Service Management Controls to Ensure
Compliance with Purchase Specification Requirements for Ground Beef.*
01099-0031-Hy. Washington, D.C.: September 7, 2005.

Monitoring of CACFP Providers in Minnesota. 27010-0018-Ch. Chicago,
IL: October 28, 2005

*Controls Over the Minnesota Department of Education's Use of Federal
Funds.* 27010-0019-Ch. Chicago, IL: June 22, 2005.

*Agricultural Marketing Service: Contract and Competitive Bidding
Practices.* 01601-0001-KC. Washington, D.C.: January 31, 2005.

Food and Nutrition Service: Controls Over USDA-Donated Commodities.
27601-0033-Ch. Washington, D.C.: September 30, 2004.

*Food and Nutrition Service: National School Lunch Program, Unified
School District 480, Liberal, Kansas.* 27010-0022-KC. Kansas City, MO:
September 30, 2004.

---

[4]Report also discusses information contained under Title I – Commodity Programs.

*Chicago SFA's Accountability and Oversight of the NSLP, SBP, and
CACFP Supper.* 27010-0017-Ch. Chicago, IL: September 30, 2004.

*Food and Nutrition Service: Compliance with Improper Payments
Reporting Requirements.* 27601-0032-Ch. Washington, D.C.: September
28, 2004.

*Food and Nutrition Service: Summer Food Service Program, State of
Nevada.* 27099-0031-SF. San Francisco, CA: August 24, 2004.

*Controls Over USDA Donated Commodities For the Year Ended June 30,
2004.* 27601-0011-SF. San Francisco, CA: August 6, 2004.

Food and Nutrition Service: Vendor Sanction Policies. 27002-0001-At.
Atlanta, GA: July 15, 2004.

*Food and Nutrition Service: National School Lunch and Breakfast
Programs Attendance and Meal Count Analysis: Philadelphia School
Food Authority, Philadelphia, Pennsylvania.* 27010-0031-Hy. Beltsville,
MD: June 25, 2004.

*Summary of Audit Results, Continued Monitoring of EBT System
Development – State of New Jersey.* 27099-0065-Hy. Beltsville, MD:
May 21, 2004.

*Food and Nutrition Service: National School Lunch Program: Kearney R-I
School District, Kearney, Missouri.* 27010-0020-KC. Kansas City, MO:
May 11, 2004.

*Food and Nutrition Service: National School Lunch Program: Platte
County R-III District, Platte City, Missouri.* 27010-0021-KC. Kansas City,
MO: April 15, 2004.

*Food and Nutrition Service: National School Lunch Program: Unified
School District 497, Lawrence, Kansas.* 27010-0014-KC. Kansas City,
MO: March 26, 2004.

*Accountability and Oversight of the National School Lunch Program –
San Lorenzo Unified School District For the Year Ended June 30, 2003.*
27099-0024-SF. San Francisco, CA: March 26, 2004.

*Food and Nutrition Service: National School Lunch Program: Unified
School District 257, Iola, Kansas.* 27010-0015-KC. Kansas City, MO:
March 26, 2004.

*Food and Nutrition Service: National School Lunch Program: Unified
School District 341, Oskaloosa, Kansas.* 27010-0017-KC. Kansas City,
MO.: March 26, 2004.

*Food and Nutrition Service: Continued Monitoring of EBT System
Development, State of New Mexico.* 27099-0018-Te. Temple, TX: March
18, 2004.

*Food and Nutrition Service: Special Supplemental Nutrition Program for
Women, Infants, and Children, State of New York.* 27099-0062-Hy.
Beltsville, MD: March 8, 2004.

Food Stamp Employment and Training Program – California.
27099-0023-SF. San Francisco, CA: February 19, 2004.

*Food and Nutrition Service: National School Lunch Program, Unified
School District 453, Leavenworth, Kansas.* 27010-0016-KC. Kansas City,
MO: February 18, 2004.

*Food and Nutrition Service, National School Lunch Program: Odessa R-
VII School District, Odessa, Missouri.* 27010-0019-KC. Kansas City, MO:
February 18, 2004.

*Food and Nutrition Service: Accountability and Oversight of the National
School Lunch Program in Texas.* 27010-0005-Te. Temple, TX: January
23, 2004.

Bellwood SFA's Administration of the National School Lunch Program.
27010-0016-Ch. Chicago, IL: December 3, 2003.

*Food and Nutrition Service: Accountability and Oversight of the National
School Lunch Program: Star Programs, Inc., Ingram, Texas.*
27010-0009-Te. Temple, TX: October 9, 2003.

Title V: Credit	*American Recovery and Reinvestment Act, Direct Farm Operating Loans (Phase 2).* 03703-0002-Te. Washington, D.C.: January 13, 2011.
	FSA Farm Loan Security. 03601-0018-Ch. Washington, D.C.: August 10, 2010.
	American Recovery and Reinvestment Act – Direct Farm Operating Loans (Phase 1). 03703-0001-Te. Washington, D.C.: February 25, 2010.
	Farm Service Agency: Controls Over Emergency Loans Reductions for Duplicate Benefits. 03601-0013-SF. Washington, D.C.: December 15, 2009.
	Controls Over Guaranteed Farm Loan Interest Rates and Interest Assistance. 03601-0017-Ch. Washington, D.C.: September 29, 2008.
	Farm Service Agency: Debt Forgiveness Restrictions on Borrower Eligibility for Farm Loan Programs. 03016-0002-Te. Washington, D.C.: March 31, 2006.
	Minority Participation in Farm Service Agency's Programs. 03601-0011-At. Washington, D.C.: November 17, 2005.[5]
Title VI: Rural Development	*Rural Development: American Recovery and Reinvestment Act – Business and Industry Guaranteed Loans - Phase 2.* 34703-0002-Te. Washington, D.C.: February 13, 2012.
	Controls Over Eligibility Determinations for SFH Guaranteed Loan Recovery Act Funds (Phase 2). 04703-0002-Ch. Washington, D.C.: September 30, 2011.
	Rural Cooperative Development Grant Program Eligibility and Grant Fund Use for a Missouri Entity. 34004-0001-KC. Kansas City, MO: August 25, 2011.
	Audit of a Rural Rental Housing Management Company Located in Indiana. 04601-0020-Ch. Washington, D.C.: May 19, 2011.

[5]Report also discusses information contained under Title XIV – Miscellaneous.

Controls Over Rural Housing Service Disaster Assistance Payments. 04601-0019-Ch. Washington, D.C.: February 7, 2011.

Rural Business-Cooperative Service: Review of Lender with Business and Industry Guaranteed Loans. 34099-0008-Te. Washington, D.C.: December 27, 2010.

Rural Utilities Service Controls Over Water and Waste Disposal Loans and Grants. 09601-0001-At. Washington, D.C.: September 30, 2010.

Rural Business-Cooperative Service: Review of Lender with Business and Industry Guaranteed Loan in Louisiana. 34099-0011-Te. Washington, D.C.: September 29, 2010.

Single-Family Housing Direct Loans Recovery Act Controls – Phase II. 04703-0002-KC. Washington, D.C.: September 24, 2010.

Rural Utilities Service: Rural or Native Alaskan Village Grants. 09099-0002-SF. Washington, D.C.: September 9, 2010.

Controls Over Rural Community Facilities Direct Loan and Grant Program Recovery Act Activities - Phase 1. 04703-0001-Hy. Washington, D.C.: June 29, 2010.

Rural Business-Cooperative Service: Review of Lender with Business and Industry Guaranteed Loan in Maryland. 34099-0009-Te. Washington, D.C.: June 24, 2010.

American Recovery and Reinvestment Act – Business and Industry Guaranteed Loan Program (Phase 1). 34703-0001-Te. Washington, D.C.: March 31, 2010.

Controls Over Recovery Act Rural Business Enterprise Grants. 34703-0001-KC. Washington, D.C.: March 31, 2010.

Review of Lender with Business and Industry Guaranteed Loan in Virginia. 34099-0010-Te. Washington, D.C.: December 29, 2009.

Review of Lender with Business and Industry Guaranteed Loan in Louisiana. 34099-0012-Te. Washington, D.C.: December 29, 2009.

Single-Family Housing Direct Loans Recovery Act Controls – Phase I. 04703-0001-KC. Washington, D.C.: November 5, 2009.

Controls Over Eligibility Determinations for Single Family Housing Guaranteed Loan Recovery Act Funds. 04703-0001-Ch. Washington, D.C.: September 30, 2009.

Multi-Family Housing Loans in Texas. 04099-0212-Te. Temple, TX: August 25, 2009.

Controls Over Lender Activities in the SFH Guaranteed Loan Program. 04601-0017-Ch. Washington, D.C.: July 2, 2009.

Request Audit of Oklahoma Rural Rental Housing Management Company. 04099-0211-Te. Temple, TX: April 28, 2009.

Rural Utilities Service: Broadband Loan and Loan Guarantee Program. 09601-0008-Te. Washington, D.C.: March 31, 2009.

Rural Utilities Service: Texas Community Connect Grantee Close-out Audit. 09601-0006-Te. Washington, D.C.: July 3, 2008.

Rural Utilities Service: Implementation of Loan and Grant Programs That Promote Renewable Energy. 09601-0007-Te. Washington, D.C.: March 21, 2008.

Rural Housing Service: Guaranteed Rural Rental Housing Program - Bond Financing. 04099-0106-SF. Washington, D.C.: March 18, 2008.

Rural Development's Single-Family Housing Force Placed Insurance Program. 04099-0139-KC. Washington, D.C.: September 28, 2007.

Rural Development: Lender's Origination and Servicing of a Guaranteed Rural Rental Housing Loan - State of Mississippi. 04601-0009-SF. Washington, D.C.: September 28, 2007.

Rural Housing Service: Controls over Single Family Housing Grants and Loans. 04601-0016-Ch. Washington, D.C.: September 25, 2007.

Controls over Single Family Housing Funds Provided for Hurricane Relief Efforts. 04601-0015-Ch. Washington, D.C.: March 30, 2007.

Improper Payments: Monitoring the Progress of Corrective Actions for High-Risk Programs in Rural Housing Service. 04601-0014-Ch. Washington, D.C.: March 20, 2007.

*Rural Business-Cooperative Service: Business and Industry Direct Loan,
Lehigh Coal and Navigation Company.* 34004-0008-Hy. Beltsville, MD:
January 31, 2007.

Guaranteed Rural Housing Loan Program Followup. 04601-0003-At.
Washington, D.C.: September 29, 2006.

*Controls Over Multi-Family Housing Funds Provided for Hurricane Relief
Efforts.* 04601-0013-Ch. Washington, D.C.: September 28, 2006.

*Rural Housing Service: Single-Family Housing Program, Borrower
Income Verification Procedures.* 04099-0341-At. Washington, D.C.:
August 14, 2006.

*Rural Business-Cooperative Service: Value-Added Agricultural Product
Market Development Grant Program.* 34601-0004-KC. Washington, D.C.:
July 28, 2006.

Community Facilities Program. 04601-0004-At. Washington, D.C.:
June 22, 2006.

Rural Rental Housing Loan Prepayment and Restrictive Use Agreements.
04601-0012-Ch. Washington, D.C.: April 14, 2006.

*Rural Utilities Service's Progress To Implement the Improper Payments
Information Act of 2002.* 09601-0001-Ch. Washington, D.C.:
March 7, 2006

*Rural Housing Service's Progress To Implement the Improper Payments
Information Act of 2002.* 04601-0011-Ch. Washington, D.C.:
February 24, 2006.

*Rural Business-Cooperative Service's Progress to Implement the
Improper Payments Information Act of 2002.* 34601-0004-Ch.
Washington, D.C.: February 8, 2006.

Rural Utilities Service: Broadband Grant and Loan Programs.
09601-0004-Te. Washington, D.C.: September 30, 2005.

*Rural Business-Cooperative Service: Request Audit of Business and
Industry Loan in Arkansas.* 34099-0007-Te. Temple, TX:
September 29, 2005.

Single-Family Housing Program in South Carolina. 04099-0340-At. Atlanta, GA: August 31, 2005.

Rural Development: Water Grants to the City of Frostburg, Maryland. 09099-0003-Hy. Beltsville, MD: June 14, 2005.

Rural Housing Service: Subsidy Payment Accuracy In Multi-Family Housing Program. 04099-0339-At. Washington, D.C.: March 23, 2005.

Rural Development: Compliance with the Improper Payments Information Act of 2002. 04601-0010-Ch. Washington, D.C.: January 27, 2005.

Rural Business-Cooperative Service: Television Demonstration Grant Program. 34099-0001-Hy. Washington, D.C.: September 30, 2004.

Rural Housing Service: Rural Rental Housing Project Management. 04016-0001-Ch. Washington, D.C.: September 30, 2004.

Rural Rental Housing Program: Housing Development Corporation, Cairo, Illinois. 04099-0143-Ch. Washington, D.C.: September 30, 2004.

Rural Development: Local Governments' Management of Multi-Family Housing Projects in North Carolina. 04004-0004-At. Atlanta, GA: July 15, 2004.

Accuracy of Single Family Housing Borrower Accounts. 04601-0009-Ch. Washington, D.C.: June 30, 2004.

Rural Business-Cooperative Service: Value-Added Agricultural Product Market Development Grant Program. 34601-0003-KC. Washington, D.C.: April 23, 2004.

Rural Development's Escrow Process for Single Family Housing Borrowers. 04601-0008-Ch. Washington, D.C.: February 2, 2004.

Rural Development: Audit of the Housing Authority of the City of Moultrie, Georgia. 04010-0001-At. Atlanta, GA: January 9, 2004.

Title VII: Research and Related Matters	*USDA's Response to Colony Collapse Disorder.* 50099-0084-Hy. Washington, D.C.: January 20, 2012.
	Controls over Genetically Engineered Animal and Insect Research. 50601-0016-Te. Washington, D.C.: May 31, 2011.
	Cooperative State Research, Education, and Extension Service – 1994 Land-Grant Institutions. 13011-0003-At. Washington, D.C.: August 17, 2007.
	Cooperative State Research, Education, and Extension Service's Progress to Implement the Improper Payments Information Act of 2002. 13601-0001-Ch. Washington, D.C.: February 8, 2006.
	Animal and Plant Health Inspection Service, Controls Over Issuance of Genetically Engineered Organism Release Permits. 50601-0008-Te. Washington, D.C.: December 8, 2005.[6]
	Cooperative State Research, Education, and Extension Service Compliance with the Improper Payments Information Act of 2002. 13601-0002-At. Washington, D.C.: January 7, 2005.
Title VIII: Forestry	*Forest Service, Forest Legacy Program.* 08601-0056-SF. Washington, D.C.: April 20, 2011.
Title IX: Energy	*Implementation of Renewable Energy Programs in USDA.* 50601-0013-Ch. Washington, D.C.: August 14, 2008.
	Implementation of Renewable Energy Programs in Rural Business-Cooperative Service. 34601-0005-Ch. Washington, D.C.: July 3, 2008[7].
	Cooperative State Research, Education, and Extension Service's National Research Initiative Competitive Grants Program. 13601-0001-Hy. Washington, D.C.: May 30, 2008.[8]

[6]Report also discusses information contained under Title X- Horticulture and Organic Agriculture.

[7]Report also discusses information contained under Title VI-Rural Development.

[8]Report also discusses information contained under Title VII-Research and Related Matters.

Commodity Credit Corporation: Bioenergy Program. 03601-0025-KC. Washington, D.C.: January 18, 2008.

Title X: Horticulture and Organic Agriculture

Agricultural Marketing Service: National Organic Program – Organic Milk. 01601-0001-Te. Washington, D.C.: February 27, 2012.

Oversight of the National Organic Program. 01601-0003-Hy. Washington, D.C.: March 9, 2010.

United States Department of Agriculture: Controls over Importation of Transgenic Plants and Animals. 50601-0017-Te. Washington, D.C.: December 12, 2008.[9]

Agricultural Marketing Service's National Organic Program. 01001-0002-Hy. Washington, D.C.: July 14, 2005.

Pesticide Data and Recordkeeping Programs. 01099-0028-At. Washington, D.C.: May 2, 2005.

Controls Over Plant Variety Protection and Germplasm Storage. 50601-0006-Te. Washington, D.C.: March 4, 2004.

Title XI: Livestock

Implementation of Country of Origin Labeling. 01601-0004-Hy. Washington, D.C.: August 18, 2011.

Animal and Plant Health Inspection Service: Administration of the Horse Protection Program and the Slaughter Horse Transport Program. 33601-0002-KC. Washington, D.C.: September 30, 2010.

Assessment of the U.S. Department of Agriculture's Disaster Response Capabilities. 42099-0004-HQ. Washington, D.C.: August 30, 2010.

USDA's Controls Over Animal Import Centers. 33601-0011-Ch. Washington, D.C.: August 13, 2010.

[9]Report also discusses information contained under Title XI-Livestock.

Food Safety and Inspection Service: Oversight of the Recall by Hallmark/Westland Meat Packaging Company. 24601-0010-Hy. Washington, D.C.: September 30, 2009.

Animal and Plant Health Inspection Service: Controls Over Pilot Qualification and Suitability. 33099-0008-KC. Washington, D.C.: September 30, 2009.

Assessment of USDA's Controls to Ensure Compliance with Beef Export Requirements. 50601-0006-Hy. Washington, D.C.: July 15, 2009.

Followup Audit of the Management and Oversight of the Packers and Stockyards Program. 30016-0002-Hy. Washington, D.C.: June 29, 2009

Evaluation of FSIS Management Controls Over Pre-Slaughter Activities. 24601-0007-KC. Washington, D.C.: November 28, 2008.

Food Safety and Inspection Service: Recall Procedures for Adulterated or Contaminated Product. 24601-0009-Hy. Washington, D.C.: August 7, 2008.

USDA's Controls Over the Importation and Movement of Live Animals. 50601-0012-Ch. Washington, D.C.: March 31, 2008.

USDA's Implementation of the National Strategy for Pandemic Influenza. 33701-0001-Hy. Washington, D.C.: January 15, 2008.

Issues Impacting Development of Risk-Based Inspection at Meat and Poultry Processing Establishments. 24601-0007-Hy. Washington, D.C.: December 4, 2007.

Food Safety and Inspection Service: State Meat and Poultry Inspection Programs. 24005-0001-At. Washington, D.C.: September, 19, 2006.

Animal and Plant Health Inspection Service: Oversight of Avian Influenza. 33099-0011-Hy. Washington, D.C.: June 12, 2006.

Assessment of USDA's Controls for The Beef Export Verification Program for Japan. 50601-0011-HQ. Washington, D.C.: February 16, 2006.

Grain Inspection, Packers and Stockyards Administration's Management and Oversight of the Packers and Stockyards Programs. 30601-0001-Hy. Washington, D.C.: January 10, 2006.

Food Safety and Inspection Service: Oversight of the 2004 Recall by Quaker Maid Meats, Inc. 24601-0004-Hy. Washington, D.C.: May 18, 2005.

Animal and Plant Health Inspection Service: National Cooperative State/Federal Bovine Tuberculosis Eradication Program. 33099-0005-Ch. Washington, D.C.: April 20, 2005.

Animal and Plant Health Inspection Service, Oversight of the Importation of Beef Products from Canada. 33601-0001-Hy. Washington, D.C.: February 14, 2005.

Animal and Plant Health Inspection Service: Exotic Newcastle Disease Eradication Project, Cooperative/Reimbursable Agreements. 33099-0010-SF. Washington, D.C.: January 20, 2005.

Animal and Plant Health Inspection Service: Wildlife Services, Aircraft Acquisition. 33099-0001-KC. Washington, D.C.: September 30, 2004.

Animal and Plant Health Inspection Service and Food Safety and Inspection Service: Bovine Spongiform Encephalopathy (BSE) Surveillance Program - Phase I. 50601-0009-KC. Washington, D.C.: August 18, 2004.

Animal and Plant Health Inspection Service: Wildlife Services' Controls Over Hazardous Materials Inventory. 33001-0005-Hy. Washington, D.C.: July 21, 2004.

Food Safety and Inspection Service: Effectiveness Checks for the 2002 Pilgrim's Pride Recall. 24601-0003-Hy. Washington, D.C.: June 29, 2004.

Food Safety Inspection Service: Oversight of the Listeria Outbreak in the Northeastern United States. 24601-0002-Hy. Washington, D.C.: June 9, 2004.

| Title XII: Crop Insurance and Disaster Assistance Programs | *Citrus Crop Indemnity Payments from Hurricane Wilma in Florida.* 05099-0029-At. Washington, D.C.: September 7, 2011. |
| | *USDA Payments for 2005 Citrus Canker Tree Losses.* 50099-0046-At. Washington, D.C.: March 23, 2011. |

*Risk Management Agency: Activities to Renegotiate the Standard
Reinsurance Agreement.* 05601-0005-KC. Washington, D.C.:
August 27, 2010.

*Risk Management Agency: Pasture, Rangeland, and Forage Pilot
Program.* 50601-0018-Te. Washington, D.C.: August 27, 2010.

Risk Management Agency: Group Risk Crop Insurance. 05601-0014-Te.
Washington, D.C.: March 30, 2010.

Risk Management Agency: Compliance Activities. 05601-0011-At.
Washington, D.C.: September 16, 2009.

Risk Management Agency: 2005 Emergency Hurricane Relief Efforts.
05099-0028-At. Washington, D.C.: March 4, 2009.

*Use of National Agricultural Statistics Service County Average Yields for
the Group Risk Protection Plans of Insurance.* 05601-0004-KC.
Washington, D.C.: March 4, 2009.

*Risk Management Agency: Crop Loss and Quality Adjustments for
Aflatoxin-Infected Corn.* 05601-0015-Te. Washington, D.C.:
September 30, 2008.

*Risk Management Agency's Improved Financial Management Controls
Over Reinsured Companies.* 05099-0111-KC. Washington, D.C.:
October 23, 2007.

Risk Management Agency: Asian Soybean Rust. 05099-0113-KC.
Washington, D.C.: June 26, 2007.

*Risk Management Agency and Farm Service Agency: Zero Acreage
Reporting Compliance.* 50099-0051-KC. Washington, D.C.:
March 28, 2007.

*Risk Management Agency: Citrus Indemnity Determinations Made for
2004 Hurricane Damages in Florida.* 05099-0027-At. Washington, D.C.:
March 26, 2007.

Risk Management Agency: Adjusted Gross Revenue Program.
05601-0004-SF. Washington, D.C.: January 23, 2007.

Risk Management Agency: New Crop Products Submitted by Private Companies. 05601-0013-Te. Washington, D.C.: February 13, 2006.

Risk Management Agency: Prevented Planting Payments For Cotton Due to Failure of the Irrigation Water Supply in California and Arizona, Crop Year 2003. 05099-0011-SF. Washington, D.C.: November 9, 2005.

Risk Management Agency: Survey of Pilot Programs. 05601-0012-Te. Washington, D.C.: May 24, 2005.

Cotton Crop Insurance: Premium Rates. 05601-0007-At. Washington, D.C.: February 10, 2005.

Risk Management Agency: Renegotiation of the Standard Reinsurance Agreement. 05099-0109-KC. Washington, D.C.: January 27, 2005.

Farm Service Agency: Apple Market Loss Assistance Payment Program. 03601-0012-SF. Washington, D.C.: June 4, 2004.[10]

Risk Management Agency: Added Land Policy. 05099-0025-At. Washington, D.C.: May 21, 2004.

Risk Management Agency: Established Maximum Price Elections for Agricultural Crops for 2001 and 2002 Crop Years. 05099-0017-KC. Washington, D.C.: March 31, 2004.

Risk Management Agency: Review of Written Agreements. 05601-0011-Te. Washington, D.C.: December 30, 2003.

Title XIII: Commodity Futures

No USDA Office of Inspector General reports issued between October 1, 2003 and February 29, 2012 related to this title.

---

[10]Was in 2002 Farm Bill Title X – Miscellaneous, under Disaster Assistance. This would correspond to Title XII in the 2008 Farm Bill.

Title XIV, Miscellaneous	*Food Emergency Response Network.* 24601-0006-At. Washington, D.C.: March 22, 2011.

Food Emergency Response Network. 24601-0006-At. Washington, D.C.: March 22, 2011.

Controls Over APHIS Licensing of Animal Exhibitors. 33601-0010-Ch. Washington, D.C.: June 29, 2010.

Animal and Plant Health Inspection Service: Animal Care Program, Inspections of Problematic Dealers. 33002-0004-SF. Washington, D.C.: May 14, 2010.

Farm Service Agency: Socially Disadvantaged Borrower Foreclosures – Farm Program Loans. 03601-0049-Te. Washington, D.C.: June 8, 2009.

Controls Over Permits to Import Agricultural Products. 33601-0009-Ch. Washington, D.C.: October 26, 2007.

USDA Homeland Security Initiatives and Directives. 50701-0002-KC. Washington, D.C.: March 12, 2007.

Review of Customs and Border Protection's Agriculture Inspection Activities. 33601-0007-Ch. Washington, D.C.: February 21, 2007.

Animal and Plant Health Inspection Service: Evaluation of the Implementation of the Select Agent or Toxin Regulations, Phase II. 33601-0003-At. Washington, D.C.: January 17, 2006.

APHIS Animal Care Program Inspection and Enforcement Activities. 33002-0003-SF. Washington, D.C.: September 30, 2005.

Animal and Plant Health Inspection Service: Evaluation of the Implementation of the Select Agent or Toxin Regulations, Phase I. 33601-0002-At. Washington, D.C.: June 23, 2005.

Review of Export Licensing Process for Animal and Plant Health Inspection Service Listed Agents and Toxins. 33601-0004-At. Washington, D.C.: March 31, 2005.

Animal and Plant Health Inspection Service: Transition and Coordination of Border Inspection Activities Between USDA and DHS. 33601-0005-Ch. Washington, D.C.: March 31, 2005.

Biosecurity Grant Funding, Controls Over Biosecurity Grant Funds Usage. 50099-0017-KC. Washington, D.C.: February 17, 2005.

Security Over Animal and Plant Health Inspection Service's Owned and Leased Aircraft. 33601-0001-At. Washington, D.C.: September 14, 2004.

Controls Over Chemical and Radioactive Materials at U.S. Department of Agriculture Facilities. 50601-0009-At. Washington, D.C.: March 24, 2004.

Followup Report on the Security of Biological Agents at U.S. Department of Agriculture Laboratories. 50601-0010-At. Washington, D.C.: March 8, 2004.

Homeland Security Issues for USDA Commodity Inventories. 50099-0013-KC. Washington, D.C.: February 23, 2004.[11]

Title XV: Trade and Tax Provisions	*Farm Service Agency: Hurricane Relief Initiatives: Livestock Indemnity and Feed Indemnity Programs.* 03601-0023-KC. Washington, D.C.: February 2, 2009.[12]

[11]Report also discusses information contained under Title I-Commodity Programs.

[12]Report also discusses information contained under Title XII-Crop Insurance and Disaster Assistance Programs.

Appendix IV: GAO Contact and Staff Acknowledgments

GAO Contact	Lisa Shames, (202) 512-3841, or shamesl@gao.gov
Staff Acknowledgments	In addition to the individual named above, Susan Offutt, Chief Economist; Thomas M. Cook, Assistant Director; Kevin S. Bray; Christine Feehan; Andy Finkel; Joy Labez; Kathy Larin; Katie Mauldin; Thomas Melito; Barbara J. El-Osta; Anne Rhodes-Kline; Cindy Saunders; William B. Shear; Carol Herrnstadt Shulman; and Phillip Thomas made key contributions to this report.

GAO's Mission	The Government Accountability Office, the audit, evaluation, and investigative arm of Congress, exists to support Congress in meeting its constitutional responsibilities and to help improve the performance and accountability of the federal government for the American people. GAO examines the use of public funds; evaluates federal programs and policies; and provides analyses, recommendations, and other assistance to help Congress make informed oversight, policy, and funding decisions. GAO's commitment to good government is reflected in its core values of accountability, integrity, and reliability.
Obtaining Copies of GAO Reports and Testimony	The fastest and easiest way to obtain copies of GAO documents at no cost is through GAO's website (www.gao.gov). Each weekday afternoon, GAO posts on its website newly released reports, testimony, and correspondence. To have GAO e-mail you a list of newly posted products, go to www.gao.gov and select "E-mail Updates."
Order by Phone	The price of each GAO publication reflects GAO's actual cost of production and distribution and depends on the number of pages in the publication and whether the publication is printed in color or black and white. Pricing and ordering information is posted on GAO's website, http://www.gao.gov/ordering.htm. Place orders by calling (202) 512-6000, toll free (866) 801-7077, or TDD (202) 512-2537. Orders may be paid for using American Express, Discover Card, MasterCard, Visa, check, or money order. Call for additional information.
Connect with GAO	Connect with GAO on Facebook, Flickr, Twitter, and YouTube. Subscribe to our RSS Feeds or E-mail Updates. Listen to our Podcasts. Visit GAO on the web at www.gao.gov.
To Report Fraud, Waste, and Abuse in Federal Programs	Contact: Website: www.gao.gov/fraudnet/fraudnet.htm E-mail: fraudnet@gao.gov Automated answering system: (800) 424-5454 or (202) 512-7470
Congressional Relations	Katherine Siggerud, Managing Director, siggerudk@gao.gov, (202) 512-4400, U.S. Government Accountability Office, 441 G Street NW, Room 7125, Washington, DC 20548
Public Affairs	Chuck Young, Managing Director, youngc1@gao.gov, (202) 512-4800 U.S. Government Accountability Office, 441 G Street NW, Room 7149 Washington, DC 20548